A FIELD GUIDE TO LEFT-WING WACKOS

A FIELD GUIDE TO
LEFT-WING WACKOS

AND WHAT TO DO ABOUT THEM

Kfir Alfia and **Alan Lipton**

SENTINEL

SENTINEL

Published by the Penguin Group

Penguin Group (USA) Inc., 375 Hudson Street, New York, New York 10014, U.S.A. • Penguin Group (Canada), 90 Eglinton Avenue East, Suite 700, Toronto, Ontario, Canada M4P 2Y3 (a division of Pearson Penguin Canada Inc.) • Penguin Books Ltd, 80 Strand, London WC2R 0RL, England • Penguin Ireland, 25 St Stephen's Green, Dublin 2, Ireland (a division of Penguin Books Ltd) • Penguin Books Australia Ltd, 250 Camberwell Road, Camberwell, Victoria 3124, Australia (a division of Pearson Australia Group Pty Ltd) • Penguin Books India Pvt Ltd, 11 Community Centre, Panchsheel Park, New Delhi – 110 017, India • Penguin Group (NZ), 67 Apollo Drive, Rosedale, North Shore 0745, Auckland, New Zealand (a division of Pearson New Zealand Ltd.) • Penguin Books (South Africa) (Pty) Ltd, 24 Sturdee Avenue, Rosebank, Johannesburg 2196, South Africa

Penguin Books Ltd, Registered Offices:
80 Strand, London WC2R 0RL, England

First published in 2007 by Sentinel,
a member of Penguin Group (USA) Inc.

1   3   5   7   9   10   8   6   4   2

Copyright © Kfir Alfia and Alan Lipton, 2007
All rights reserved

Photographs courtesy of ProtestWarrior LLC unless otherwise indicated.

Drawings by Philip Awry

LIBRARY OF CONGRESS CATALOGING-IN-PUBLICATION DATA
Alfia, Kfir, 1974-
A field guide to left-wing wackos : and what to do about them /
Kfir Alfia and Alan Lipton.
p.   cm.
Includes index.
ISBN 978-1-59523-037-9
1. Liberalism—United States—Humor. 2. Protest movements—
United States—Humor. I. Lipton, Alan, 1974- II. Title.
PN6231.L47A44 2007
818'.602—dc22   2006035781

Printed in the United States of America

Set in Plantin with Melvinsans
Designed by Daniel Lagin

To Jenny,
Who told me to stop complaining and do something about it

CONTENTS

A FIELD GUIDE TO LEFT-WING WACKOS

INTRODUCTION

Congratulations, reader! You have taken the first step toward being able to identify correctly the eighteen major species of liberal protesters. After reading this book, you will possess the knowledge you need to defend yourself against the swarming pests the liberal media refer to as demonstrators. You will become a ProtestWarrior like us, and, we hope, have a few laughs along the way.

But before we go any further, a little background on who we are and how we came to write this book.

We are two ordinary young Americans. Kfir Alfia was born in Israel in 1974 and moved to Dallas with his family when he was three. Alan Lipton was born in Dallas, also in 1974. We met in our first-grade Hebrew class and have been best friends ever since. Throughout our school career, our common interest in film and politics led us to a number of collaborations, including a public access political call-in show and a feature-length screenplay.

Our paths diverged when we headed off to that land of liberal learning known as college. Kfir graduated from the University of Texas at Austin and Alan graduated from Syracuse University.

We reconnected in San Francisco.

For us, San Francisco was an eye-opener. It was a town so liberal that the street people had more rights than the taxpayers. During the months leading up to the Iraq War, we were shocked at the intolerance and stupidity of the daily protests filling the streets. We supported the war effort, but our voices of support were drowned out by the screaming, hysterical cries of the antiwar movement that surrounded us. We were suffocating in left-wing smog.

We were frustrated by the swirling political rhetoric that gained so much attention but made so little sense. We knew we had to do something to maintain our own sanity and to expose the dangerous ideological forces behind the noisy left-wing nonsense.

So, in March 2003, our astonishment turned to action and we launched ProtestWarrior.

As field researchers, we followed in the footsteps of Bronislaw Malinowski and Roger Tory Peterson and went on safari into the heart of liberal demonstrations. We discovered that left-wingers were much like other wildlife. Different groups of liberal protesters exhibited patterns that made them distinguishable by their appearance, their habitats, and even their calls.

As we learned to distinguish the different species, we discovered something more disturbing. Different species of left-wingers used protests to lend new legitimacy to long-discredited and otherwise unpopular political movements.

We discovered that left-wingers used protests to take refuge from the harsh light of rational discourse and nourish their egos in the lenses of fawning television cameras. Liberal protesters realize they cannot compete in the marketplace of ideas, so they work in the marketplace of the media.

What shocked us even more than discovering the real political beliefs of the liberal protesters was that the media refused to identify these radicals for who they really were. Mesmerized by the bright colors and catchy slogans, the media covered the protests through rose-colored lenses.

Like Jane Goodall among the apes, we continued our studies.

We ventured further into the wilds of the American political landscape, notebooks and cameras in hand, to learn who these people were and what they were up to. The protests offered us a rare opportunity to see left-wingers in their unalloyed perversity.

We identified the left-wingers by their bizarre appearance. We visited their habitats. We recorded their cries. We walked up to left-wingers and started talking to them. We took their premises to their logical illogical conclusions. We punctured their moral self-righteousness. We showed them that the policies they endorsed actually led to what they were protesting against. With our acute powers of perception, and by just standing around a lot, we pierced the heart of liberal darkness.

In all of our investigations, we have always followed strict rules of nonviolence and respect for the rights of others. Despite our friendly manner, the liberal protesters were uniformly uncooperative. As we started to get our own media attention, liberal dislike for us morphed into outright hostility. The protesters became vicious, nasty, and intolerant, far different from the peaceful do-gooders portrayed in the media.

Left-wingers spat on us, shouted us down, destroyed our signs (see Appendix for example ProtestWarrior signs), and assaulted us. Challenging left-wingers during a demonstration became as dangerous as feeding the bears in Yellowstone National Park. Left-wingers seemed cute and cuddly, but they would rip your head off if you gave them a chance.

Today, ProtestWarrior is America's leading antiactivist activist group (visit us at www.protestwarrior.com). ProtestWarrior chapters have been set up in all fifty states, as well as in countries around the world. ProtestWarrior includes individuals from all walks of life and all parts of the country, thirteen thousand strong. Our membership includes college students and military veterans, executives and soccer moms—thinking people of all ages and backgrounds. There are hundreds of ProtestWarrior chapters spread out all across the world—in Canada, England, Argentina, Israel, Holland, and even France.

With the information contained in the following pages, you will be able to identify the eighteen major species of left-wing protesters quickly and easily.

So read on, ProtestWarriors.

And take it to the streets.

ANARCHISTS

MAKESHIFT FLAG POLE (TRI-FOLD TENT FRAME)
READY FOR SPONTANEOUS SHOW OF SOLIDARITY

MANDATORY GLARE COUNTERS
HANDKERCHIEF'S HOWDY DOODY LOOK

GESTURE TO ALERT FLOCK TO
STARBUCKS STOREFRONT

INSTANT COMMUNICATION
WHEN IT'S TIME TO "BLOC UP"

$249.99

CHAPTER I

|||||||||||||||||||||||||||||||||||||||||||||||||||||

ANARCHISTS

Anarchist: Someone who advocates the abolition of the state, private property, and anything else that prevents him from feeling good about himself. Like a political two-year-old, he will throw a fit if he doesn't get what he wants—or throw bombs instead.

PROTESTING THE PROTESTERS

Small Band of Conservatives Comes to Town to Answer Anti-Bush Groups
By Robert MacMillan
washingtonpost.com Staff Writer
Thursday, January 20, 2005; 5:59 PM

Ten minutes after telling his fellow protesters to stay safe, Gil Kobrin lay huddled in the slush and mud as two anarchists repeatedly kicked him in the back.

How he got from point A to point B is simple enough. Kobrin, accompanied by a dozen members of the conservative group ProtestWarrior, crashed a rally of hundreds of anti-Bush demonstrators at Meridian Park in Washington, D.C. Holding aloft signs that read "Say no to war unless a Democrat is president" and "Not to brag, but Bush won, so shove it!" they had set off earlier on inauguration morning in search of their opposites.

The ProtestWarrior contingent didn't have to search for very long; the party came to them.

"You can go a [expletive] half-mile away and stand on the first street corner you see!" shouted a self-described anarchist, dressed all in black with a bandana covering his face. As they taunted and threatened and liberally profaned Kobrin and the rest of the group, a member of the D.C. Anti-War Network (DAWN)—the official organizers of the rally—tried to break it up.

"Your purpose is to instigate people. You're going to have to leave!" shouted the "marshal," DAWN's term for their ad hoc security force.

"We're staying here," Kobrin replied.

Then he went down under a hail of black boots. Once the marshals pulled the anarchists away, ProtestWarrior sued for peace and made for the exit.

IDENTIFYING CHARACTERISTICS

Anarchists are widely regarded by conservatives as the intellectual scum of the leftist underworld. Typically recruited at a very young age, these creatures travel in herds (typically called "blocs") and boast a very strict dress code. But behind this seemingly stylish postapocalyptic neo-bank-robber look lie very practical reasons for each and every fashion choice and accessory. Because anonymity is their overriding fashion principle, the great lengths Anarchists go to remain anonymous often end with very entertaining results.

Baseball caps are a favorite, and will afford them the shade and cover they so desperately crave. Rarely will you find any type of insignia emblazoned on the front, since it would most likely represent a business entity, anathema to our Anarchist specimen. Colors other than black and dark blue are rare.

The hat is often coupled with the bandana (Figure 1.1), once a fa-

Figure 1.1: Bandana

Figure 1.2: Balaclava

vorite among trick-or-treating bandits from the fifties, which has been brought back into vogue by this species.

Primarily this is useful for them in concealing their identity, but it also serves as a crude protection against tear gas attack. An Anarchist has to scowl pretty hard to overcome the utter absurdity of the bandana face mask. Since most specimens fail to do so, observing Anarchists in the wild is often a treat. However, after years of being confronted with this dilemma, many Anarchists have opted to use the balaclava (Figure 1.2) as a means of hiding their identity.

Many prefer to keep one in their backpack while they wear the bandana, as a more anonymous mask will be needed when they start to "bloc up." Ever resourceful, Anarchists can transform a T-shirt into a makeshift balaclava (Figure 1.3).

Although it is very rare for an Anarchist to sport any brand of clothing, their allegiance to Dickie's brand jackets and pants defies this principle, as it is almost an exclusive accessory. Dickie's, a very union-friendly manufacturer, is a necessity if you claim to be a friend of the working man, which, of course, all Anarchists are.

An Anarchist will almost exclusively wear a black T-shirt to go with the ensemble. If the T-shirt has any design at all, it will mostly likely be nondescript—no brand names, of course. To round off the apparel, thick black boots are a must, but to stay cool during the summer, Converse hightops are preferred.

It is not uncommon to find Anarchists carrying a cell phone in their Dickie's pant pocket. Like their fellow-traveler Communists and

Figure 1.3: Makeshift balaclava

Islamothugs, they have no problem using technologies made possible only by Western-style capitalism and property rights to serve their purposes. Track cell phones are highly preferred, allowing them to make phone calls without leaving a paper trail—a must if you want to organize activities under the police's radar.

If the Anarchist is active in the circle, he will most likely have a backpack, chock full of practical items such as spray paint, crystal meth, and books on do-it-yourself munitions. The backpack also stores his fold-up tent pole, which can quickly be attached to their black flag (Figure 1.4) if a spontaneous show of solidarity and rebellion is called for.

THE ORIGIN OF THE SPECIES

First named as a political species by William Godwin in 1793, Anarchists have appeared in Russia, France, and the United States. They were particularly popular in the late nineteenth century, when they realized the attempted assassination of German emperor William I (1878), the Haymarket bombing in Chicago that killed eight policemen and dozens of laborers (1886), the assassination of President Sadi Carnot of France (1894), the assassination of Empress Elizabeth of Austria (1898), the assassination of King Humbert I of Italy (1900), and the assassination of U.S. President McKinley (1901). Anarchists made a surprisingly strong showing at the World Trade Organization meeting in Seattle in 1999, where they used hockey sticks to fire tear gas canisters back at the police. Anarchists may be vegetarians, naturopaths, nudists, or Esperanto speakers. They may describe themselves as evolutionary Anarchists, revolutionary Anarchists, Communist Anarchists, individual Anarchists, philosophical anarchists, anarchafeminists, and anarchosyndicalists, but George Bernard Shaw probably got it right when he observed, "Anarchism is a game at which the police can beat you."

Although continual rejection by mainstream society is a crucial ingredient in the making of an Anarchist, what separates Anarchists from their intellectual cousins the Communists (besides lots of black clothing) is a hyperinflated sense of superiority. Add some bad childhood grounding experiences, a heap of unpaid parking tickets, and a nihilistic rejection of the intellect, and you're well on your way to understanding this species' psychological underpinnings.

BEHAVIOR

Observing a lone Anarchist in the wild is extremely rare and has never been documented. During a protest, Anarchists will travel in herds, moving in an agitated and liquid state, much faster than the other species found at a protest. A spontaneous grouping together of disparate smaller groups of Anarchists is called a "huddle" and is usually followed

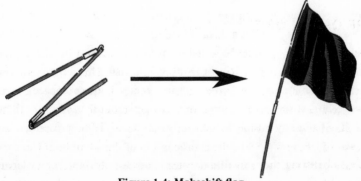

Figure 1.4: Makeshift flag

Meet Emma, anarchy's Grandma. But don't get too cuddly—in 1892 she plotted to murder Henry Frick, a steel industrialist, and had her boyfriend carry it out. Frick survived, but was shot three times and stabbed twice with a poisoned knife. She even incited a Polish émigré to assassinate William McKinley. To modern Anarchists, this is cause for some serious street cred.

by a spirited display of property damage (any readily available icon of capitalism is fair game, with Starbucks being the target of choice). A group of four or more are called a "collective," a "direct action" group up to eight is called a "krew," and any group larger than twenty is called a "mob."

If you find yourself near a mob, it is highly advisable to seek shelter, as it is the signaling of an imminent "bloc" activity. Not to say that Anarchists are by any means dangerous—this is more of an issue of staying away from the tear gas when the police move in to neutralize our enthusiastic specimens. It has been hypothesized that Anarchists are slowly becoming immune to tear gas and new, more powerful strains are evolving.

HABITAT

This species can be found in the more metropolitan areas of the United States and Europe, with a disproportionately high concentration of Anarchists in the Bay Area. Now, while at first it might seem that the Bay Area's notoriously high cost of living would make for a harsh environment for Anarchists to thrive in, this species is quite content to live meagerly and has found many ways to get around paying for things. Stealing from any business is not only condoned, it's considered a public service.

As befitting their revolt against any sort of structure or order, the

Anarchist breed is largely decentralized, with little in the way of organized leadership. They generally operate as independent cells, many of which might be run out of their parents' basement.

Anarchists will migrate en masse toward Republican National Conventions and G-8 meetings. Scientists have not yet discovered what biological mechanism causes such orderly patterns of migration, but it is hypothesized that Anarchists have an innate biological attraction to events involving people in power and find these travels cathartic, as nothing makes an Anarchist happier than causing violence, forcing the police to respond, and thus justifying their fantasy visions about the repression of capitalist society.

CALL OR SLOGAN

The commodity is the opium of the people.
The more you consume the less you live.

THE PARTY LINE

Anarchy will revolutionize the world as we know it, offering mankind complete liberation from work, breaking down all barriers of authority so that man can live and share the earth harmoniously and cooperatively. In the Anarchist world, you will be free to do as you wish as no man-made barriers will be there to thwart you, and no one will hurt you as it would be against man's true instinct to do so.

BETWEEN THE LINES

Anarchist philosophy is boilerplate Marxism without the fancy economic mechanics. If they were truly just against "man-made barriers," they would appreciate American constitutionalism and hate the rigidity of Communist and Islamic societies. Of course, just the opposite is true, as Anarchists like to sneak in at the end of the sales pitch that all private property will be abolished. Their utopian vision is that when our society adopts anarchism everyone will voluntarily surrender their property to the public and there will be little if any need for use of force. Those who insist on owning the products of their labor will be dealt with, since according to anarchism, *all* property is theft. Implicit in this view is the notion that once all vestiges of civilization have been destroyed and we have been reduced to the level of savages, there will no longer be good or bad or any standards of objective merit, and the human race will finally be liberated in total equality.

IN THEIR OWN WORDS

"The Sling Shot—It is cheap, legal to carry, silent, fast-loading and any right size rock will do for a missile. A few hours of shooting stones at cans in the back yard or up on the roof will make you marksman enough for those fat bank windows and even fatter pigs."

—Abbie Hoffman in *Steal This Book*

REQUIRED READING

Powell, William. *The Anarchist Cookbook* (1970). An Anarchist classic, that has nothing to do with politics but a lot to do with drugs and bombs. Chapters include "Drugs: From Pot to Hydrangea Leaves" and "Explosives and Booby Traps: From How to Make Nitroglycerine to Cacodyl."

BEST OF BREED

- Pierre Joseph Proudhon (1809–65)—Successful French Anarchist who helped lead thirty thousand Frenchmen to their deaths in the Paris Revolution of 1848. Favorite quotation: "Property is robbery."
- Mikhail Bakunin (1814–76)—Russian Anarchist who split with Karl Marx over the need for a transitional workers' state and the proper recipe for borscht.
- Ya Basta—European Anarchist group present at the November 1999 World Trade Organization protest in Seattle, whose padded white overalls made them look like anarchist Michelin men (and women).
- The Angry Brigade—Group of London Anarchists who succeeded in bombing the home of the British home secretary in 1971 and later bombed the home of the managing director of Ford in London.

HANDLING TIPS

- *Level One (couch commando)*—If you spot a stray Anarchist, ask him to explain how an anarchist society would actually work. Since he rarely gets confronted with such questions, the Anarchist will likely seek refuge among the rest of his anarchist mob.
- *Level Two (fairly concerned citizen)*—Hand out balaclavas with the eyes sewn shut to less affluent Anarchists.
- *Level Three (ProtestWarrior)*—During a protest, put a mock Starbucks sign on the local police headquarters' window. Anarchists will instinctively gather and will eventually throw a brick through the window. The Anarchists will be arrested and placed in jail, making it easier for the police to keep track of them.

COMMUNISTS

CHAPTER 2

||||||||||||||||||||||||||||||||||||||||||||||||||||||||||||||||||

COMMUNISTS

Communist: Anyone who likes the things you have, wants them for his own, and doesn't mind if a totalitarian state is what it takes to make that happen.

IDENTIFYING CHARACTERISTICS

Communists are considered the Maytag repairmen of liberal protesters, few and far between but somehow still devoted to a profoundly lost cause. Even after the ocean of blood that has been spilled implementing the core tenet "From each according to his ability to each according to his need," this twisted species is undaunted and marches on without a moment's pause, making them the True Believers of the leftist underworld.

Communists love to talk theory—how a single political party (the Communist Party) must control the means of production and the distribution of wealth in order to create a classless society. They are absolutely certain that the "dictatorship of the proletariat" is inevitable, that capitalism will crumble, and that all wealth will be communally owned. The Communist will say all these things, and believe them fervently, even when confronted with the facts that communism has been a disastrous failure wherever it's been tried and has caused incalculable misery around the world. Many experts have determined that Communists manage to maintain their relentless determination for the simple reason that they are clinically insane.

Another identifying characteristic of Communists is their severe inferiority complex. An ideology that promises an equal standard of living regardless of ability, merit, or effort is going to attract two types of people, both equally despicable: the parasite and the luster after power. The parasite longs for the state of complete abrogation of responsibility, where he can be taken care of by those who are forced to provide him with his basic needs like a place to live, a nice job, or that new Blu-ray DVD player. The luster after power intuits that the redistribution of wealth requires a redistributor, and he is only too happy to assume this crucial role. Both refuse to live by their own effort, and require the involuntary cooperation of others.

Sometimes mumbling, sometimes yelling, sometimes gesticulating wildly, sometimes separating themselves in quiet isolation, Communists are as unpredictable as they are irrational, making it entertaining to identify them.

THE ORIGIN OF THE SPECIES

Being a Communist in America today is not for the faint of heart. While it may have been stylish to be a card-carrying member of the Communist Party in decades past, the word "Communist" today is little more than a synonym for "loser." The Communist species appeared on the scene long before communism was considered the vanguard of political thought, with the birth of the German philosopher Karl Heinrich Marx in 1818. Marx, a freelance journalist and egghead extraordinaire, eventually developed an analytical method called historical materialism, the basic thesis of which was that "the nature of individuals depends on the material conditions determining their production." In other words, all of history can be interpreted as the struggle between laborers and capitalists. Marx concluded that the capitalists by their nature force the workers into soul-crushing servitude and exploitation, but you have to get a Ph.D. at an Ivy League university to understand why—you see, it's very, very complicated.

Figure 2.1: Historical materialism in action

Karl ran amok with this new theory and became obsessed with framing every aspect of the universe in terms of class struggle. Determined to impress his European ivory tower contemporaries, he formulated an economic and moral critique of capitalism that forecast a worldwide economic collapse, to be replaced by a revolutionary cooperative utopia. Marx managed to convince himself and many other influential intellectuals that in a capitalist market, profit (which he called "surplus value") was solely derived from "surplus labor," which was the difference between the amount of workers' labor that goes into a product and the amount of labor necessary to produce the means of livelihood of the worker. Thus Marx concluded that the laborer would always get the sucker deal in a capitalist economy, and if the control over the means of production were to be wrested away from the capitalist class and into the hands of the workers, oh, what a wonderful world it would be. But of course, Marx noted, the capitalists would resist such a transition, and therefore the transformation to a Communist system might require quite a bit of bloodshed. Fortunately the world was safe from Marx's harebrained ideas during his lifetime, and it remained just political conjecture until three decades after his death.

It was under the direction of Bolshevik leaders Nikolai Lenin and Leon Trotsky that Communist theory was finally implemented in 1917 in Russia, and Marx's prediction that "violent revolution would in general be required" became the understatement of the century. All private property was nationalized, and the workers were finally in the saddle. But instead of delivering the cooperative utopia promised by Marxist theory, the Bolsheviks introduced the world to the monstrous slave pen they liked to call a "planned economy." Early Communist leaders were quick to realize that only the most brutal regime could preside over a nation where citizens were stripped of their rights. In the end Joseph Stalin, whom Trotsky called "the outstanding mediocrity in the party," proved to be the most savage of those competing for control of the newly formed gang-ruled government, and it was during his ascension to power that the world first witnessed the truly ugly nature of this Marxist "Noble Experiment." In order to remain in power, Stalin had all of his political opponents murdered, imprisoned, or sent to labor camps. Peasants who resisted the collectivization of agriculture were shot, sent to the Gulag, or deported to remote areas of the country to starve to death. Under Stalin's Five-Year Plan, areas that did not meet production targets had their grain taken away, and peasants were forced to remain in starving areas, resulting in an estimated ten million deaths. Soviet Russia proved to the world that it was possible to create a fully cooperative society, since all uncooperative citizens disappeared.

It was during Stalin's heyday that Communist theory found a home in America among academics and intellectuals. Safely removed from the wreckage of these implemented theories, they lent their moral support and discussed the possibility of introducing this radical social system in America. Thus, the U.S. Communist Party was born. At the bidding of the Soviet leadership, American Communists helped lead early labor riots and organized powerful industrial unions. A Communist candidate ran for political office every year from 1924 to 1984, with the same result—big losses. In 1968, the Communist candidate for U.S. president got only 438 votes. (Even Americans in that decade weren't too keen on moving to a totalitarian system.) By the 1970s, U.S. Communists managed to eliminate themselves from political influence due to continuous infighting, and the party almost disappeared with the collapse of the Soviet Union in the late 1980s. Since the Soviet Union had bankrolled the American Communist Party for more than forty years, this proved to be the final nail in the CPUSA coffin.

BEHAVIOR

Communists are not a very happy species and look at the world with dejected eyes. They must struggle with the thought that every day, people around the globe get up, go to work for themselves or for a private company, and then spend their money at the shop or the market—all anathema to a Communist. Constantly confronted with the fact that their ideology has led to prison camps wherever it has been implemented, Communists avoid the moral dilemma by ascribing the abhorrent living conditions of Communist countries to the failures of the leadership ("That wasn't communism, that was Stalinism!" "If they had followed Trotsky's interpretation of Marx it would have worked!" "Of course it was a disaster—their spirit of cooperation was half-hearted!," and so on). However, many Communists find relaxation and respite in daydreaming that one day when the revolution comes, they will be able to dictate to those who now have everything (see Figure 2.2).

Today's Communists have little imagination and like to be told what to do. Only there are no Communist figures left to tell them what to do. Some still hang on to the shining example of Cuba as the Communist ideal. Others are trying to cling to China, even though the Chinese Communist Party does not want to have anything to do with them. In desperation, some American Communists have recently gone "mainstream," as when Sam Webb, the current head of the Communist Party U.S.A., threw the support of the Communist Party behind some Democratic candidates in 2004.

When the few sad, lonely, embittered Communists do get together, they bicker among themselves about highly abstruse aspects of Communist political theory, such as whether it was Leninism, Trotskyism, or Stalinism that was the true implementation of Marxist doctrine, or

Figure 2.2
"Once the socialist revolution happens, THEN THEY'LL RESPECT ME."

the various options available to Communists in the area of facial hair. Communists spend most of their time dealing with endless meetings, listening to boring philosophical dissertations on class struggle, "direct action," and passing out ragged copies of the *People's Weekly World* periodical. According to the Communist Party platform, all members are expected "to attend their club meetings (which range from twice a month to less frequently where there are great distances involved), pay dues (a minimal fifty cents to one dollar a month), read and circulate our press, raise money to support the PWW and the work of the party, and participate to the best of their ability in other party activities." This life of "social action" and "struggle" makes for an abysmal existence, which is why suicide rates and conversion into mixed-market capitalist is frequent among this species.

HABITAT

One can find Communists at the rally area of a protest, setting up booths, lining up their "literature," or sitting Indian-style on the floor hawking their manifestos.

The best place to find Communists away from a liberal protest is at the Communist Party headquarters, located at 235 West 223rd Street in New York City, New York. It is speculated that one can find the majority of the entire U.S. Communist population gathering at this tiny location during weekends. Every once in a while, a Communist sympathizer will actually visit a Communist country, eager to witness his comrades realizing his ideals. However, he soon discovers that few Communists can be found even in Communist countries and is baffled at the number of citizens expressing their desire to get the hell out. Hollywood is another great place to find Communists—not real Communists but fictional ones. According to Hollywood, Communists are comic book heroes who always helped the downtrodden (instead of killing them). Before he played Dick Tracy, Warren Beatty paid homage to American Communist Party founder John Reed in the epic film *Reds*. Countless big-name films tell the saga of the freedom-fighting unfairly blacklisted Hollywood Ten (see Hollywood Activists chapter), such as *The Way We Were* (1973, starring Robert Redford and Barbra Streisand), *The Front* (1976, starring Woody Allen), *Guilty by Suspicion* (1991, starring Robert De Niro), *The Majestic* (2001, starring Jim Carrey), and *One of the Hollywood Ten* (2001, starring Jeff Goldblum). These Hollywood sympathizers ignore the fact that Communist states are brutal totalitarian killing machines, even though the Communist leaders may live a Hollywood lifestyle. Steven Spielberg, Oliver Stone, Jack Nicholson, Kevin Costner, and other fawning Hollywood heavies have made pilgrimages to Cuba to spend a lavish evening and smoke cigars with the island's iron-fisted dictator while thousands of political prisoners languish behind bars.

SIGNS AND SLOGANS

Workers of the World, Unite!
Death to Capitalism—Abolish Private Property!

THE PARTY LINE

Modern industry has converted the little workshop of the patriarchal master into the great factory of the industrial capitalist.

Masses of labourers, crowded into the factory, are organised like soldiers. . . . Not only are they slaves of the bourgeois class, and of the bourgeois State; they are daily and hourly enslaved by the machine, by the over-looker, and, above all, by the individual bourgeois manufacturer himself. . . .

You are horrified at our intending to do away with private property. But in your existing society, private property is already done away with for nine-tenths of the population; its existence for the few is solely due to its non-existence in the hands of those nine-tenths. You reproach us, therefore, with intending to do away with a form of property, the necessary condition for whose existence is the non-existence of any property for the immense majority of society. . . .

In one word, you reproach us with intending to do away with your property. Precisely so; that is just what we intend.

—Karl Marx and Friedrich Engels, *The Communist Manifesto*

BETWEEN THE LINES

Do you ever daydream at work about how much better a job you could do than your idiot boss? When you see well-to-do citizens, do you feel that they have not toiled nearly enough to deserve their possessions? Are you afraid to learn new marketable skills or confused about how to accumulate capital? Do you want to be respected by your peers, regardless of your ability or personality? Well, my friends, then communism might be the cure-all you've been looking for! In just a few years and one violent government overthrow, you could be part of the socially just country you've always dreamed of. Your boss will find himself working in the trenches by your side. Or better yet, you might be able to turn the tables on him and show him what it's like to be under *your* heel! The once-wealthy citizens you so despised will be forced to have their possessions redistributed to the public—and you'll get a piece of the action! And job skills? Why worry about job skills when you can get paid just for getting up in the morning? And don't forget the instant respect (and fear) you'll command as you move up the ruling party's ranks (don't worry, the lower your character the faster you'll rise). So remember to vote communism, and you'll never have to worry about voting ever again!

IN THEIR OWN WORDS

Death solves all problems—no man, no problem.

—Joseph Stalin

Ideas are more powerful than guns. We would not let our enemies have guns, why should we let them have ideas.

—Joseph Stalin

In the Soviet army it takes more courage to retreat than advance [speaking on the Soviet policy of gunning down all soldiers suspected of desertion and unauthorized retreat].

—Joseph Stalin

Gaiety is the most outstanding feature of the Soviet Union.

—Joseph Stalin

There are no absolute rules of conduct, either in peace or war. Everything depends on circumstances.

—Leon Trotsky

HANDLING TIPS

- *Level One (couch commando)*—Make a living and buy things. Living a capitalist life drives Communists batty.

- *Level Two (fairly concerned citizen)*—Ask a Communist who his favorite Communist dictator is. Hard-pressed to think of one who hasn't been responsible for murdering thousands of dissidents, he will panic and begin to sputter about how communism has never been properly implemented.
- *Level Three (ProtestWarrior)*—Bring a fellow ProtestWarrior who has fled from a Communist regime along to a liberal protest and have him carry a sign that says, "I lived in a Communist country and it sucked. Ask me how." Introduce yourselves to some Communists at their booth and get your friend to share his experiences with them. Since Communists instinctually evade anything that might contaminate the floating abstractions in their heads, and they can't leave the booth and their literature, this will be the equivalent of electroshock therapy.

INTELLECTUALS

CHAPTER 3

||||||||||||||||||||||||||||||||||||||||||||||||||||||||||||||||||||||||||||||||||

INTELLECTUALS

Intellectual: The spiritual leaders of the left, Intellectuals give lectures and write arcane tracts on political analysis with the sole purpose of providing protesters with the assurance that their hatred of America is thoroughly justified.

IDENTIFYING CHARACTERISTICS

Intellectuals form the philosophical intelligentsia of the leftist movement. These Ivy League–tenured pedagogues are usually very small in stature and extremely unsightly. After spending a lifetime having to come to terms with their severe bodily shortcomings, most Intellectuals opt to spend their entire lives in the forgiving world of academia. All too aware of their own glaring physical limitations, these specimens are usually ardent champions of socialism, and consider the self-made man to be their archnemesis.

Although they claim radical sympathy with the working class, Intellectuals wear clothes that recall the campus geek look of the 1960s. This is understandable, since most of them were campus geeks in the 1960s. Houndstooth jackets, button-down shirts, dull brown ties, battered leather shoes, even a threadbare blazer are commonly worn by the Intellectual. Women Intellectuals tend toward flowing skirts or ill-fitting jackets. And glasses. The true mark of an Intellectual is glasses—the thicker the better. It's rare to see an Intellectual at a protest. Often they are not in good enough shape to actually march in a protest march. If they do attend, they are usually among the first to arrive, the first speakers to address the protest rally, and the first ones to leave. Or the Intellectual may be too busy to protest because he is working on a documentary about himself and his great intellectual discoveries.

Whether Intellectuals attend a protest or not, their presence is always felt. Behind every vitriolic slogan accusing the United States of being the *real* terrorist threat, behind every T-shirt calling Bush a war criminal, behind every banner demanding totalitarian third-world countries' right to "self-determination," lies an embittered Intellectual, spewing ferociously anti-American venom posing as informed political analysis.

THE ORIGIN OF THE SPECIES

The Intellectual has been around as long as there have been politics, although the American baby-boom generation has more Intellectuals than any other group in history. The founding of the United Nations in 1945 marked a hyperextension of Intellectuals throughout the planet. Suddenly, Intellectuals didn't need academia or the lecture circuit to support their pontificating lifestyle. They could live in New York City and publish endless studies for the United Nations on everything from Global Warming to U.S. human rights violations.

Since the 1960s, American universities have become the breeding ground and the feeding trough for Intellectuals. The Intellectuals of today were once militant College Students (see Chapter 4) engaging in campus protests and storming the faculty offices. However, instead of leaving behind the world of angst and radical politics to get a job in the private sector, they have preferred to stay in the protected environment of the ivory tower. Here, they can think in peace and concentrate on formulating their radical socialist leanings into an academically accredited curriculum—a curriculum they will use to "educate" the incoming generation of students.

BEHAVIOR

Intellectuals are distracted, worried, continuously depressed and upset by the state of world affairs. They are utterly convinced that the "military-industrial complex" is in full swing with the help of a complicit corporate-controlled media keeping the masses from discovering the real truth. Why are they the only ones who can see it so clearly? In their state of constant anxiety, Intellectuals develop compulsive behavior patterns that include scribbling random notes in their notebooks, carrying around arms full of "important" documents, giving intimate "off the cuff" lectures to young, eager acolytes, yelling at their TV during news segments, and obsessively recording themselves on video.

One of the most interesting Intellectual behavior patterns is that they rarely make public statements about the subjects in which they are trained. They make profound and sweeping statements about the global economy, human rights, the environment, and international politics even though they teach linguistics or art history. And when they do talk or publish essays about their arcane area of expertise, such as "generative grammar analyses" or "contemporary gender roles in advertising," their audience consists of a handful of fellow eggheads and captive TAs.

Intellectuals are very thin-skinned and prone to acerbic outbursts when challenged, especially during class. Anyone who doesn't share their world view of the destructive "Western Hegemony" is accused of racism, sexism, or classism, and will be put on the Intellectual's mental list, to be used later when assessing final exam grades.

Intellectuals are most happy when there's a protest going on right on their own campus. Whatever the cause—workers' rights, antiwar, anticorporate, or removing ROTC and military recruiters from campus—as long as it bears the official "progressive" markings, they will enthusiastically support it and will feel a surge of pride in their ideological influence on campus politics. Of course, they won't actually attend the rally, but they will take the time to write an impassioned letter-to-the-editor to the campus newspaper praising the courageous activists who had the

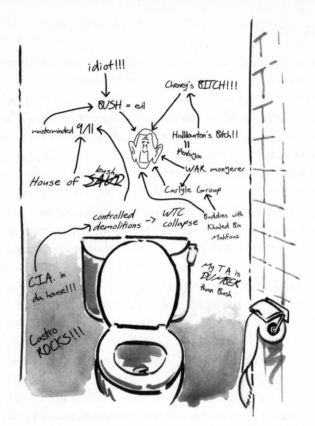

Figure 3.1: Intellectual faculty restroom at Ivy League university

character to stand up for what they believed in, and damn it, that's what this country so desperately needs right now.

Intellectuals take great pride in their fearlessness for making controversial statements in class or during interviews—statements they feel everyone else is just too scared to say, such as claiming that America is the biggest purveyor of evil in the modern world, or stating that 9/11 was a completely natural retaliation by heretofore powerless Muslim victims acting out of frustration from years of American meddling and aggression, or praising totalitarian Communist dictators' refusal to give in to Western domination. Being the only one to bring up such offensive and preposterous points, an Intellectual fancies himself a modern-day Copernicus. And anyone who questions the validity of his claims is just one of the many millions of Americans being bamboozled by the duplicitous media.

Intellectuals love to talk about the so-called propaganda model of the American mass media. You see, our media are actually a tightly controlled branch of the government, in which every news story is calculated to mobilize public opinion that serves America's "ruling class," all the while deluding the public into thinking that freedom of the press actually exists. But leave it to the clairvoyant and brilliant Intellectuals to see right through the vicious facade and explain things as they really are. However, when it comes to explaining how it is they get their share of media attention (if their ideas are so dangerously exposing the truth), or explaining the proliferation of independent Internet media outlets, Intellectuals are finally quick to shut up.

HABITAT

The libraries at college campuses are the natural habitat of the Intellectual, who is continually researching the most critical issue of modern times—how many times they are mentioned in the press. Intellectuals who have actual academic positions can usually be found in the various "studies" departments of the university—American Studies, Womyn's Studies, Gay and Lesbian Studies, Black Studies, Latin-American Studies, Environmental Studies, Jewish Studies. This campus environment is perfectly suited for their emotional and intellectual development and allows the Intellectual to devise political theories while safely detached from the stubborn reality of the outside world. For instance, most Intellectuals like to espouse socialism as a political ideal and actually admit that the Soviet Union was a brutal and tyrannical regime. However, like most apologists of socialism, they consider the U.S.S.R. a betrayal of socialism, not an implementation of it. And the suffering and death of millions of Russians under Soviet rule bothers them only in that these historical calamities have tarnished socialism's otherwise sterling reputation. This insulating theoretical campus environment also allows them to carry on, undeterred, even though every other socialist state is always headed by an aggressive, backward, and repressive centralized government—the very traits they claim to denounce.

Some Intellectuals who find the cushy walls of the ivory tower a bit too deadening seek refuge from reality in left-wing "think tanks." This is where they get paid quite handsomely to examine, verify, and conclude whatever it is the think tank needs to warrant more government or foundation grant funding.

Many Intellectuals inhabit a world of "alternatives"—alternative lifestyles, alternative histories, and alternative realities. One alternative to getting a job is to be kept as a "house Intellectual" by a wealthy liberal, either a movie star with political ambition, like Rob Reiner, or a bored billionaire like George Soros. Wealthy liberals enjoy the company of Intellectuals who are willing to pander to their charitable whims— delivering research papers and cowriting books that definitively prove whatever it is the wealthy liberal wants to have proved.

SIGNS AND SLOGANS

Celebrate Diversity
Resist American Hegemony!

IN THEIR OWN WORDS

Any dictator would admire the uniformity and obedience of the U.S. media.

—Noam Chomsky

Everybody's worried about stopping terrorism. Well, there's a really easy way: stop participating in it.

—Noam Chomsky

The Bible is one of the most genocidal books in history.

—Noam Chomsky

The overriding goal of American policy has been to construct a system of societies that are open to free economic intervention by private enterprise.

—Noam Chomsky

Plans are being made and programs implemented on the assumption that they may lead to the death of several million people in the next couple of weeks . . . very casually with no comment, no particular thought about it, that's just kind of normal, here and in a good part of Europe.

—Chomsky's prediction of a "silent genocide" that would happen in Afghanistan if the United States intervened there after 9/11

As a Ph.D. Islamologist and Arabist I really hate to say this, but I'll say it anyway: 9/11 had nothing to do with Islam. The war on terror is as phony as the latest Osama bin Laden tape.

—Kevin Barrett, associate lecturer at the University of Wisconsin– Madison and enthusiastic member of the "Scholars for 9/11 Truth" (Barrett has also asserted that other purported terrorist at- tacks, including the July 7, 2005, London bombing, and the March 11, 2004, Madrid bombing, were the actions of a "special wing of, probably, U.S. or Western military intelligence")

Palestinians who have resorted to necessary killing have been right to try to free their people, and those who have killed themselves in the cause of their people have indeed sanctified themselves.

—Ted Honderich, professor of the philosophy of mind and logic at University College London and author of *After the Terror*

The government has been lying to us about 9/11 from scratch. . . . There is no "hard evidence" Osama was involved. What we have found, I regret to say, leads in the direction of implicating some of the highest officials of our own government in treason and mass murder.

—James H. Fetzer, professor emeritus, University of Minnesota– Duluth, on the U.S. government's orchestration of the 9/11 at- tacks (controlled demolition from the top down) for political and

economical gain. Fetzer also asserts that all of the hijackings were
staged and even calls from passengers to relatives were faked.

They found that by creating a nation, a symbol, a legal unity called
the United States, they could take over land, profits and political
power from the favorites of the British Empire. In the process,
they could hold back a number of potential rebellions and create a
consensus of popular support for the rule of a new, privileged
leadership.

—Howard Zinn on the founding of America by English
immigrants *(A People's History of the United States)*

The Industrial Revolution and its consequences have been a disaster for the human race. They have greatly increased the life-
expectancy of those of us who live in "advanced" countries, but
they have destabilized society, have made life unfulfilling and have
subjected human beings to indignities, have led to widespread
psychological suffering . . . and have inflicted severe damage on
the natural world.

—Ted Kazynski, from his manifesto
"Industrial Society and Its Future"

REQUIRED READING

A People's History of the United States (1980). Howard Zinn's alternative fiction about the history of the United States that celebrates all the people
in the United States, except the guys who get up and go to work every
day.

Hegemony or Survival: America's Quest for Global Dominance (2003). Chomsky's attempt at convincing the public that not only does the United
States fund terror regimes when it's in America's interest, but the repression of other nations' citizenry is in fact the very reason Americans
support certain foreign leaders. If you find yourself instinctively recoil-
ing from such a morally preposterous claim, Chomsky will tell you that
it's proof of how effective the American propaganda machine has
become.

The New York Times. Read the editorial page any day to get the latest on cutting-edge Intellectual thought.

BEST OF BREED

- Upton Sinclair (1878–1968)—Sinclair was a muckraking novelist who took on every "social justice" issue he could to try to sell a book. His most famous novel, *The Jungle* (1906), was written to try to teach the public about the evils of capitalism using the U.S. meat-packing industry as a background. His book didn't start a socialist revolution, but it did lead to the passage of the Pure Food and Drug Act in 1906. Depressed that capitalism hadn't become reviled as he had planned, he lamented, "I aimed at the public's heart, and by accident I hit it in the stomach." Sinclair was a rare Intellectual in that he was actually willing to implement and live in his grand socialist vision. Taking the profits he made from *The Jungle*, he started a socialist commune, which promptly burned down. He experimented with telepathy, which he celebrated in the novel *Mental Radio* (1930), and ran a losing campaign for governor of California in 1934.

- Howard Zinn (b. 1922)—An American historian and political scientist who is professor emeritus in the Political Science Department at Boston University, Zinn has led the Intellectual debate that espouses Marxism, anarchism, socialism—anything but capitalism. A World War II B-17 bomber pilot, Zinn was fired from his tenured position at Spelman College, traveled to North Vietnam to protest the war, and helped edit *The Pentagon Papers* with Noam Chomsky. Although Zinn's book *A People's History of the United States* has sold more than a million copies, he has been less successful selling his three plays, *Daughter of Venus* (1985); *Emma* (1986), a celebration of the life of anarchist Emma Goldman; and *Marx in Soho* (1999), a celebration of the work of Karl Marx.

- Ward Churchill (b. 1947)—A tenured professor of ethnic studies at the University of Colorado, Ward has spent most of his career, when not actually teaching classes, obsessing over America's history of suppressing political dissent. Claiming Cherokee ancestry, he fancies himself as a one-man crusade to expose America's genocidal history and repression of Native Americans or any other group deemed subversive. Of course, Ward has always been left free to publish books and give lectures and interviews about his conspiracy theories and paranoid musings, but he's not referring to this repression—he's talking about the *other* Americans being silenced. Ward was thrown into the limelight when he published an essay after the 9/11 attacks, in which he expressed the opinion that the victims in the Twin Towers got exactly what they deserved: "They were too busy braying, incessantly and self-importantly, into their cellphones, arranging power lunches and stock transactions, each of which translated, conveniently out of sight, mind and smelling distance, into the starved and rotting flesh of infants. . . . If there was a better, more effective, or in fact any other way of visiting some penalty befitting their participation upon the little Eichmanns inhabiting the sterile sanctuary of the Twin Towers, I'd really be interested in hearing about it." And hear about it he did. In an uproar of public condemnation and allegations of academic misconduct, on May 16, 2006, his university's investigative committee on research misconduct agreed unanimously that Churchill had engaged in "serious research misconduct," including four counts of falsifying information, two counts of fabricating information, two counts of plagiarizing the works of others, improperly reporting the results of studies, and failing to "comply with established standards regarding author names on publications." He was even caught lying about his military service, claiming that he went to paratrooper school, then volunteered for Vietnam and served a ten-month tour as part of a Long Range Reconnaissance Patrol to track down North Vietnamese. But military records show that Churchill was trained as a projectionist and light truck driver and give no indication that he went to paratrooper school or trained for LRRP. In 2006, he resigned in shame from his post as chairman of ethnic studies.

- Ted Kaczynski (b. 1943)—Born to an intellectual family, Ted Kaczynski, "the Unabomber," dropped out of Harvard and lived in a cabin in the Montana wilderness without heat or electricity or plumbing.

Though he never showed up at a liberal protest, Kaczynski was a spiritual leader of the Intellectuals, a man without a college degree whose bizarre protests made headlines around the world. Kazynski wrote a thirty-five-thousand-word manifesto entitled "Industrial Society and Its Future" but couldn't get it published until he started bombing people. Fortunately, most of Kaczynski's bombs were harmlessly defused. "Frustrating," Kaczynski wrote in his journal, "but I can't seem to make a lethal bomb." Some of Kaczynski's bomb-making efforts resulted in injuries and at least three deaths—and in Kaczynski getting the *New York Times* and the *Washington Post* to publish his "work," with the encouragement of Attorney General Janet Reno. When Bob Guccione, owner of *Penthouse*, offered the Unabomber a monthly column, Kaczynski became the most successful literary terrorist in history. After his brother turned him in in 1996, Kaczynski was sentenced to life without parole but wrote in his journal, "Do not get the idea I regret what I did. I would do it all over again."

POSTER BOY

Noam Chomsky (born Avram Noam Chomsky, 1928)—"The L. Ron Hubbard of the New Left" and the institute professor emeritus of linguistics at the Massachusetts Institute of Technology, Chomsky was born in Philadelphia to Jewish immigrants from Eastern Europe and made a name for himself in the field of linguistics, whose theory of generative grammar challenged the behaviorist approach to language acquisition and dramatically influenced the philosophy of language and mind and a lot of other stuff that no one really cares about. A member of the Industrial Workers of the World and a sympathizing anarchosyndicalist, Chomsky has received honorary degrees from more than two dozen universities and is one of the world's most cited scholars, but all this has nothing to do with linguistics. What launched him into his cult hero status among the vitriolic left was his relentlessly ferocious attacks on America's history, culture, leadership, and mass media. And because his attacks are framed as seemingly dry academic analyses, he lends an authentic voice to those who had, up until then, only felt their hatred of America in their gut. Using his own unique writing method of self-reference as a cover for baseless opinions, Chomsky was able to make sweeping generalizations about America's war on terror: "The entire commentary and discussion of the so-called War on Terror is pure hypocrisy, virtually without exception. Can anybody understand that? No, they can't understand it." He has harshly criticized America's intervention in South America to establish free democracies while he romanticized brutal third-world Communist revolutionaries. He views the American public as brainwashed jingoists, completely indifferent to the damage their government, which they enthusiastically support, has wreaked around the world, and feels that 9/11 was just a logical cause-and-effect. While blaming America's foreign policy for instigating Muslim terrorist attacks, he sees terrorism as a viable political tool as long as it's pointed in the right direction: "If we are going to take a moral position on this—and I think we should—we have to ask both what the consequences were of using terror and not using terror. If it were true that the consequences of not using terror would be that the peasantry in Vietnam would continue to live in the state of the peasantry of the Philippines, then I think the use of terror would be justified." Today, Chomsky is considered to be one of the left's foremost intellectual gurus and continues to publish books, give speeches, and write articles, none of which have anything to do with linguistics.

HANDLING TIPS

- *Level One (couch commando)*—If you have a son or daughter currently deciding on which university to attend, do your due diligence and help them weed out schools infested with Intellectuals. After all, your hard-earned money should not be going to subsidize lectures accusing you of lockstep fascism.
- *Level Two (fairly concerned citizen)*—If it's too late and you're already a student with an Intellectual professor, the next time he goes into a tirade about how America, capitalism, or President Bush are the world's greatest terrorist threats, ask him where he gets his sources. If the In-

tellectual doesn't evade the question or launch into a personal attack and actually rattles off a list of sources, ask if he can cite anyone more objective—you know, someone who isn't a dyed-in-the-wool socialist, and watch him stammer and try to change the subject.

- *Level Three (ProtestWarrior)*—Attend an Intellectual's lecture while dressed in full Islamothug garb complete with suicide belt. When you cause a commotion with the lecturer and his audience, tell them not to worry, that you consider them among the few "good ones," and that you just came in for a quick pep talk before you redressed your grievances at the local shopping mall.

COLLEGE STUDENTS

CHAPTER 4

<u>|||||||||||||||||||||||||||||||||||||||||||||||||||||||||||||||||||||||||||||</u>

COLLEGE STUDENTS

College Student: A product of higher learning eager to emulate superficially the political unrest of the sixties and to express a newfound concern for stolen elections, America's failed capitalist system, and America's history of fascist aggression.

IDENTIFYING CHARACTERISTICS

College Students are the youngest of the species you will find at a protest. Motivated by all they have learned about the world from within the ivory towers, they yearn to find meaning in what they perceive to be a very privileged life. Although they are eager to emulate the spirit of dissent that erupted on college campuses in the sixties, they are too comfortable in their Nikes, Pumas, and Adidas sneakers and designer jeans to venture into the muck of an all-encompassing counterculture. Distracted by the day-to-day demands of college life and allured into activism by zealous professors, College Students choose the causes to rally behind in a whirlwind of emotionally charged dogmatic sound bites. Many of them belong to student lobby groups, such as the Gay and Lesbian Association, Muslim Student Association, or Campus Antiwar Network, and are typically majoring in a subject that contains the word "Studies" (Middle Eastern Studies, Womyn's Studies, Environmental Studies, African Studies, and so on). Many College Students spend much of their time engrossed in the study of victimology (part of the unofficial curriculum in most modern universities) and multiculturalism, seeing themselves and their peers as victims of injustice and in constant need of protection. Often encouraged by the university faculty, College Students make racial and gender issues a constant topic of discussion, as they are all too aware of the apparent racism and sexism that pervade America, their campus, and their lives. And in case it fades from their consciousness, the university is only too happy to remind them with a "Rape Awareness Week" or "Cultural Awareness Week."

THE ORIGIN OF THE SPECIES

College Student activism has been part of the campus landscape since the 1960s, when the new counterculture began to pick up steam. Students from upper- and middle-class families began to question the status quo and raised their political voices on the issues of civil rights, the Vietnam War, and free speech—causing lots of property damage along the way. While organizations like Students for a Democratic Society spun off violent groups like the Weather Underground, the college faculty and administration were bewildered at the utter turmoil brewing across their campus green. They often scrambled to ease tensions and meet the unreasonable list of demands of students hijacking their buildings. As this old guard began to retire out of their academic positions, they were replaced by the College Students of the sixties, who brought along with them a fanatical brand of political activism. While most opted to keep their agendas ulterior, some felt quite comfortable using their newfound positions in higher education to treat their campus as a testing ground for radical social transformation:

> After the Vietnam War, a lot of us didn't just crawl back into our library cubicles; we stepped into academic positions. With the war over, our visibility was lost and it seemed for a while—to the unobservant—that we had disappeared. Now we have tenure, and the work of reshaping the universities has begun in earnest.
> —English professor Jay Parini, Middlebury College

The university is institutionally racist. American society is racist and sexist. Covert racism is just as bad today as overt racism was thirty years ago. In the 1960s we were frustrated about all this. But now, we are in a position to do something about it.

—Donna Shalala, chancellor of the University of Wisconsin

Ours was the generation that took over buildings in the late 1960s and demanded the creation of Black and Women's Studies programs and now, like the return of the repressed, we have come back to challenge the traditional curriculum.

—Henry Louis Gates of Duke University

I see my scholarship as an extension of my political activism . . . to expose the myths the U.S. has always put forward about itself as an egalitarian nation. . . . The [U.S.] has taken this incredibly fertile continent and utterly destroyed it with a ravaging hatred.

—Annette Kolodny, dean of the humanities, University of Arizona

The College Students of today are the end product of this experiment in cultural transformation, and are often encouraged by their teachers and the administration to see the world as they see it. Many of these professors are "Intellectuals" (see Chapter 3) who find their biggest audience among their naive students, eager to get involved. The respect (and tuition checks) of the students give these professors the idea that they are actually doing something meaningful.

BEHAVIOR

College Students feign a constant state of indignation—at the current administration, at corporations, at the racism and sexism pervading their college campuses. Many find relief in submitting letters to the editor of their campus paper. While they admit to themselves that it's not doing much, it's better than doing nothing, and does a hell of a job of alleviating any guilt that might surface during the kegger later in the evening. Other College Students who need a more tangible outlet for their progressive angst join or start student activist groups that purport to fight the injustice of sweatshops, defend union workers, divest funds from Israel, or protect the environment and the rights of animals. Some of these activist groups are remarkably easy to organize, as they are supported by their national counterparts. For instance, to start an activist branch of PETA, all you need to do is visit their website and request a "College Action Pack" (see Figure 4.1), chock full of flyers, pamphlets, recruitment material, and strategies for milking the activist-friendly campus environment for all it's worth: "Becoming an officially recognized campus group has many advantages: You'll receive a campus mailbox; be able to use fax machines, copiers, and other office supplies; have access to campus facilities, like meeting rooms; and, most importantly, be eligible to receive funding" (PETA website).

While organizing and recruiting for leftist activist groups is the most common College Student activity, protesting military recruiters and getting them kicked off campus is a close second. College Students' antimilitary recruitment campaigns are often violent, attacking recruiters and vandalizing offices. Even off-campus recruitment offices are targets for College Students, often at the behest of their Intellectual professors who believe graduates are unable to make an informed decision to join the military.

Although College Students spend a great deal of their energy protesting in support of what they perceive as "free speech," another peculiar behavior exhibited by the College Student is shouting down and physically threatening conservative speakers invited to campus. This gives them the opportunity to create a distraction with their indignation as a cover for their absolute lack of an argument and utter intellectual bankruptcy. For example, on September 27, 2000, Dan Flynn, author of the book *Cop Killer: How Mumia Abu-Jamal Conned Millions into Believing He Was Framed* (see Chapter 6's Poster Boy), was invited to speak at UC Berkeley. Even before he arrived, hundreds of posters announcing the lecture were torn down. During his lecture, the College Students in the audience screamed "Racist!" "Nazi!" "Murderer!" while a black College Student invaded the stage and wrote www.kkk.com behind him on the chalkboard. Another College Student dropped his pants and "mooned" the speaker and then attempted to rip the mi-

Figure 4.1: Revolution in a box

crophone's cord from the wall. At the end of the lecture, a mob of College Students stole all of the copies of Dan's book and held a book-burning, while holding signs admonishing others to "Fight Racist Censorship."

Ward Connerly, the anti-Blacktivist who ended race-based admissions in California state schools, was met with similar hostility when speaking at the University of Texas at Austin. The "Anti-Racist Organizing Committee" advertised days in advance of their planned disruption and wrote a column in the campus paper urging students to show that Connerly's "rhetoric will not be tolerated" and that "at other universities, fed-up students have forced him off stage." On the day of his arrival, AROC passed out flyers around campus encouraging students to show up at the lecture for the purpose of screaming to the point where it would be impossible for anyone to hear what Connerly actually had to say. During his speech, AROC members yelled insults, pounded the walls, stomped their feet, and waved Orwellian placards, such as "Protect Free Speech—Shut Connerly Up!"

Another pastime of College Students is sacking conservative student newspaper stands. In 1997, a mob of activists stole hundreds of copies of the *Cornell Review* and held a newspaper burning at the Ithaca campus. When the conservative editors attempted to report the incident of censorship to the dean of students, they were slightly discouraged to learn that he had attended the fascist-style rally in support of the newspaper burners and smiled as the papers went up in flames. A spokeswoman for Cornell defended the rally: "The students who oppose the *Cornell Review* have claimed their First Amendment right to be able to have symbolic burnings of the *Cornell Review*."

Unfortunately for College Students, some of them actually get arrested for violence and vandalism. However, university administrators are always looking for ways to aid in this inevitability. For instance, inspired by the arrest of two student government representatives illegally disrupting a speech given by Wisconsin's governor Tommy Thompson, the student government at University of Wisconsin-Madison passed a bill that allowed mandatory university-collected student fees to be used to pay the bail of student protesters imprisoned for radical activism and civil disobedience.

HABITAT

College Students like to hang out on the campus green—a perfect protest staging area. You can also find them hanging up PETA and Socialist Student Society meeting posters at the student union.

The more ambitious College Students inhabit the offices of college newspapers and the litter-strewn studios of college radio stations, way to the left of the dial. These students sleep on ripped sofas and live off discarded pizzas and whatever other consumables they can score, while they position themselves to apply for graduate school in journalism or broadcasting.

Another favorite habitat for college student protesters is workshops. These gatherings are arranged by professors so that they can get paid to talk to themselves and recruit students to do their research and writing for them. One recent workshop was presented by the Institute for Anarchist Studies at Goddard College and entitled Renewing the Anarchist Tradition (RAT).

CALLS OR SLOGANS

War Criminal!
They're our brothers, they're our sisters, we support war resisters.

IN THEIR OWN WORDS

I am a male WASP who attended and succeeded at Choate Preparatory School, Yale College, Yale Law School and Princeton Graduate School. Slowly but surely my lifelong habit of looking, listening, feeling, and thinking as honestly as possible has led me to see that white, male-dominated, Western, European culture is the most destructive phenomenon in the known history of our planet. . . . It is deeply hateful of life and committed to death; therefore, it is moving rapidly toward the destruction of itself and most other life forms on earth. And truly, it deserves to die.

—Benjamin T. Hopkins, Chestertown, Md.,
in *Mother Jones*, December 1982

POSTER GIRL

A martyred hero of College Students worldwide, Rachel Corrie earned major street cred by getting herself killed while preventing the Israeli Defense Force from rooting out underground tunnels used by Palestinian terrorists to smuggle explosives and weapons from Egypt.

Rachel was a typical College Student—affiliated with a number of campus activist groups, including Olympia Movement for Justice and Peace (code words for pro-Intifada) and the International Solidarity Movement. However, after deciding to travel abroad after graduation, instead of going to Mexico, South America, or Europe, Rachel traveled as an activist to the town of Rafah in the Gaza Strip at the height of the Al-Aqsa Intifada. After arriving, she attended two days of training with other ISM activists where she learned how to best thwart the Israeli military from rooting out terrorist weapons and explosives smuggling tunnels. These tunnels begin on the Egyptian side of the border and are used by Hamas, Popular Front for the Liberation of Palestine, and Al-Aqsa Martyrs Brigade to arm themselves with weapons and explosives. The tunnels snake past the border and reconnect with the surface on the Palestinian side, typically inside residential homes, concealed under bathrooms, living rooms, and children's bedrooms. Hosting and maintaining smuggling tunnels can often become a family business that provides a primary source of income, and many Palestinian civilians actively aid and abet terrorist activity, making the problem of preventing such smuggling a PR nightmare.

After her "direct action" training in the Gaza Strip, she took part in a mock trial of President Bush (held by a group called the Young Palestinian Parliament) and gave "evidence" to young Palestinian children so that they, too, would find him guilty of crimes against humanity. She also took part in an anti-American demonstration where she burned a U.S. flag to the angry chants of Palestinian children.

After participating in the anti-American/Israeli pep rallies, Rachel was finally ready for the real mission. She and other members of the ISM gathered around what Israel calls "no-man's-land"—the area near the border with Egypt where Palestinian smugglers often clash with Israeli military. While the IDF bulldozers began to excavate smuggling tunnels, Rachel and the ISM crew stood in front of the bulldozers to prevent them from inching forward. When a bulldozer made contact with these activists, it would nudge them out of the way. After one of the bulldozers created a mound of dirt from the excavation, Rachel decided to stand behind the mound where the driver would not be able to see her at all. As the bulldozer continued its work, Rachel was struck by a slab of concrete resulting in her death, making her the most celebrated "useful idiot" of the Palestinian Intifada.

HANDLING TIPS

- *Level One (couch commando)*—Post a ProtestWarrior sign (which you can cut out from the Appendix) at the Student Union.
- *Level Two (fairly concerned citizen)*—If you're a student, start a Corporation Appreciation Week at your school (unofficially, if necessary). If any indignant and incredulous College Students approach, ask them to list all of the corporations directly responsible for the products the College Student uses on a daily basis, starting with their clothes.
- *Level Three (ProtestWarrior)*—The next time a conservative speaker is invited to speak at your local campus, along with a friend, take a sign with you that says I SHOUT DOWN IDEAS I DON'T AGREE WITH. As soon as the screaming hordes of College Students show up, hold the sign behind each one as your friend takes a picture and post the pictures all over campus the next day.

HOLLYWOOD ACTIVISTS

CHAPTER 5

||||||||||||||||||||||||||||||||||||||||||||||||||||||||||||||||||||||||||||||||||||||||||||||||||||||||||||||||||||

HOLLYWOOD ACTIVISTS

Hollywood Activist: A member of the Hollywood community elite who uses the capitalist fruits of wealth and fame to promote a socialist agenda.

IDENTIFYING CHARACTERISTICS

Hollywood activists are the most identifiable species of protester, since you already know them. You watch their movies, buy their CDs, and see them on TV—they are the front men and women of the entertainment world. For the most part, this species is populated by film and television actors and actresses, but it also includes film and television writers, producers, directors, musicians, artists, comedians, and other "artists."

Spotting them at a protest can be easy, as they are usually surrounded by gawking protesters. Although Hollywood activists attend protests to negate the air of elitism they feel diminishes their credibility, they will usually (depending how famous they are) be accompanied by some sort of security detail to keep them clear from the masses (Figure 5.1). Usually, a TV crew will be nearby to document their willingness to mix with the commoners, and for a possible interview. Their attire usually consists of jeans and a button-down shirt, with a T-shirt draped over, with some type of anti-Bush or anti-Republican or anticorporate message, as they are trying to fit in with the rest of the protesters.

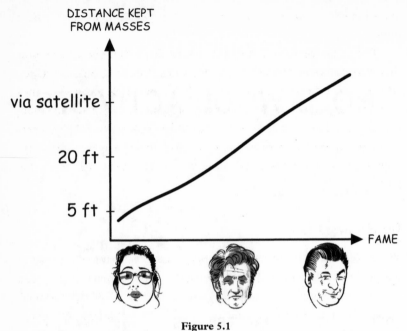

Figure 5.1

In any antiwar march, if there is a Hollywood activist present, he or she will most likely be at the head of the procession, in front of the banner, much to the protest organizers' delight.

ORIGIN OF THE SPECIES

The Hollywood activist appeared with the birth of the star system, when Florence Lawrence became the first film performer to be identified by name on screen and in film advertising. This star system made the leading men and women of the era household names and, as feared by the studios, gave these performers more leverage in their salary demands. Soon the studios learned that when releasing information to the public regarding new projects, people seemed to be more interested in details of the stars' personal lives. What were they like? What did they do for leisure? Who were they dating? Studio executives, public relations men, and agents worked together with the actor to answer these questions and to create a star persona—a persona that would help market their films.

These stars learned that their marketability was influenced by how they were perceived by the public. So they became paragons of style, elegance, and beauty, and when they spoke, people listened. But they were just normal people, with an army of publicists, agents, and studio executives at their disposal to maintain their sterling image. This characterized much of early-twentieth-century Hollywood, where stars carefully kept their controversial political affiliations hidden from the public.

The Hollywood Ten

The most famous early example of Hollywood activism is the case of the notorious "Hollywood Ten." In 1947, ten filmmakers had been cited for contempt of Congress for refusing to divulge their political affiliations to the House Un-American Activities Committee (HUAC). The HUAC was a committee set up to investigate Communist infiltration in Hollywood. Although the current delusional Hollywood community regards these filmmakers as victims, this is far from the truth. Hollywood Activists like to believe they're a constant target of political persecution. So they feign indignation that the Hollywood Ten had had their Freedom of Speech violated and were unjustly blacklisted—just for being humanitarian idealists.

These so-called humanitarians were called to testify about whether they belonged to the Communist Party. At the time, being a member of the Communist Party meant that that person had agreed to take orders to commit criminal and treasonable actions on behalf of the Communist Party and the Soviet government it served. This is the same Soviet government that was openly dedicated to the violent overthrow of the U.S. government. This very real national security risk was at the heart of why the HUAC convened to determine whether these Hollywood filmmakers were official members. The Hollywood Ten refused to say whether they were party members, which was grounds for contempt of Congress—an offense that carries a jail sentence.

Another myth surrounding these so-called Hollywood heroes was that they were unfairly and even illegally blacklisted from the Hollywood industry, when, in fact, in a bout of conscience inconceivable today, the top-tier Hollywood executives of the time met and decided to blacklist those who had refused to testify. This is a perfectly legal, fair, and reasonable reaction on the part of the executives. After all, why would these businessmen voluntarily hire someone who would use his or her position to try to eliminate all private property and private business, which is the objective of the Communist Party? More than just an act of self-preservation, boycotting those who ideologically and financially support a regime that has exterminated millions is a moral obligation.

Yet the current Hollywood community ignores these facts so that they can maintain their self-righteous posturing in the delusion that they are being muzzled.

BEHAVIOR

All Hollywood Activist behavior derives from an intense, all-consuming guilt and a belief that all good fortune (especially theirs) is entirely arbitrary and unrelated to individual merit. This massive insecurity and self-doubt leads them to the delusion that they have a duty to repre-

"THE HOLLYWOOD METAMORPHOSIS"
THE SEVEN STEPS TO BECOMING A HOLLYWOOD ACTIVIST

BEFORE THE ACTOR BECAME FAMOUS, HE TOILED
IN OBSCURITY, WAITING FOR HIS "BIG BREAK"...

STEP 1

sent the common man, the masses, the "little guy." (See "The Holly-wood Metamorphosis" for the progression of this unique psychological phenomenon.)

Hollywood Activists operate in an environment where their political opinions, no matter how preposterous, are voiced unchallenged. This is because they are completely surrounded by sycophantic admirers or other Hollywood Activists who have identical opinions. A particularly popular sentiment shared among this species is hatred of all things Republican, with Bush as their supreme boogieman.

Due to the fact that they are almost completely insulated from differing political opinions, a fully developed Hollywood Activist will often say things that are baffling to the average American. For instance, on April 15, 2003, Tim Robbins said to the National Press Club, "In the 19 months since 9/11, we have seen our democracy compromised by fear and hatred. Basic inalienable rights, due process, the sanctity of the home have been quickly compromised in a climate of fear." Regarding the 2000 Bush election victory, Alec Baldwin said, "I know that's a harsh thing to say, perhaps, but I believe that what happened in 2000 did as much damage to the pillars of democracy as terrorists did to the pillars of commerce in New York City."

Statements like these beg the question—what makes a celebrity offer such asinine opinions with apparently no thought at all? A typical public political statement by a Hollywood Activist will glaringly

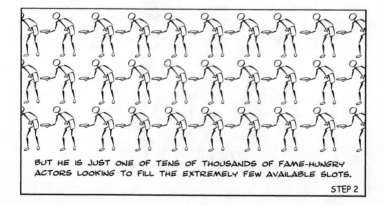

BUT HE IS JUST ONE OF TENS OF THOUSANDS OF FAME-HUNGRY ACTORS LOOKING TO FILL THE EXTREMELY FEW AVAILABLE SLOTS.

STEP 2

contradict how they conduct their personal lives. This creates some of the most entertaining and outrageous spectacles of hypocrisy known to man.

For instance, a Hollywood Activist who is fervently antigun will employ a small army of armed guards to protect her life and property. Or a star who rails against the Bush administration for stripping him of his freedom of speech will become indignant when the public exercises their freedom by not attending his movie.

HABITAT

This species is found almost exclusively in Los Angeles, California, the center of the entertainment universe. The more outspoken an activist, the more lavish his lifestyle, particularly his home. Hollywood activists typically dwell in multimillion-dollar gated asylums. This causes a serious problem with their desperate attempt to remain in touch with the common man. However, this paradox remains repressed or rationalized for practical purposes. After all, how can Hollywood Activists fight for the downtrodden if they are encumbered by pesky day-to-day discomforts?

THE PARTY LINE

We are Democrats because we believe everyone has a right to live in a fair society, free from racism, war and oppression. There are those out there who want to exploit and enslave you, and it would be a crime if we did not use our unique position to voice our opinions and shed the light of truth.

BETWEEN THE LINES (IN THEIR OWN WORDS)

One of the main purveyors of violence in this world has been this country [America], whether it's been against Nicaragua or wherever. . . . I've been an advocate for peace my whole life. But one of the main purveyors of violence in this world is this country.

— Danny Glover

And it all seems to be for him and his friends to keep getting richer at the expense of a nation, at the expense of the environment. It's like a full-scale assault on the environment.

—Gwyneth Paltrow

ONCE FAMOUS, HE IS TREATED WITH INSTANT AND INTENSE RESPECT AND ADORATION. EVERYWHERE HE GOES, PICTURES ARE TAKEN OF HIM, HE ENCOUNTERS STAR-STRUCK FANS, HE BEGINS TO DATE A BEAUTIFUL YOUNG STARLET OR MODEL, HE NEVER HAS TO WAIT IN LINE, HE'S GIVEN FREE MERCHANDISE, PEOPLE WANT TO KNOW EVERY DETAIL OF HIS LIFE NO MATTER HOW MUNDANE. SOON AN INFLATED SENSE OF HIS OWN IMPORTANCE BEGINS TO GROW.

STEP 4

The Republican Party, their message and their policies of exclusion and the tilted playing field appeals to the dumb and the mean. There is no shortage of dumb and mean people in this culture. So, therefore, their message, the dumb and the mean find a nice home in the GOP.

—Janeane Garofalo

Bush means Dick Cheney, Tom DeLay, and all these f*cking cryptofascists are gonna get in and start carving up the pie and handing in all their markers to the Republican Party that's been itching to get back into power.

—John Cusack

Republican comes in the dictionary just after reptile and just above repugnant. . . . I looked up Democrat. It's of the people, by the people, for the people.

—Julia Roberts

Alcoholics Anonymous and jazz are the only original things of importance [America] has exported to the rest of the world.

—Martin Sheen

BUT THIS SELF-IMPORTANCE IS COUNTERED BY A TREMENDOUS GUILT THAT BEGINS TO SWELL. HE KNOWS IT COULD HAVE EASILY BEEN SOMEONE ELSE TO TAKE HIS SPOT. HE IS SUBCONSCIOUSLY AWARE THAT THE RESPECT AND AWE LAVISHED BY THE MASSES IS NOT COMMENSURATE WITH HIS ABILITY. HIS TALENT IS THAT HE CAN PRETEND TO FEEL/THINK/SAY SOMETHING IN FRONT OF A CAMERA. HE WONDERS: IS THIS ENOUGH REASON TO BE TREATED LIKE ROYALTY? STEP 5

They [corporations] control culture. They control ideas. And I think the revolt of September 11th was about "F—— you! F—— your order!"

—Oliver Stone

We should look to [Castro] as one of the Earth's wisest people, one of the people we should consult.

—Oliver Stone

I think that people like the Howard Sterns, the Bill O'Reillys and to a lesser degree the bin Ladens of the world are making a horrible contribution [to society]. I'd like to trade O'Reilly for bin Laden. [O'Reilly] is a grumpy, self-loathing joke.

—Sean Penn

Let us find a way to resist fundamentalism that leads to violence. Fundamentalism of all kinds, in al-Qaeda and within our government. And what is our fundamentalism? Cloaked in patriotism and our doctrine of spreading democracy throughout the world, our fundamentalism is business.

—Susan Sarandon

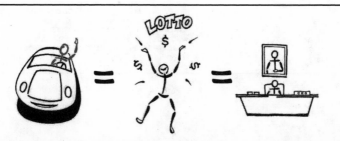

THIS GUILT THAT HIS WEALTH AND PRESTIGE WAS UNEARNED LEADS HIM TO BELIEVE THAT ALL DISPARITIES OF WEALTH HAVE ARBITRARY CAUSES. THE HAVES (LIKE HIM) ARE LUCKY AND THE HAVE-NOTS ARE UNLUCKY. HIS GUILT OVER BEING ONE OF THE FEW RECIPIENTS OF THIS TREMENDOUS LUCK LEADS HIM TO A BURNING DESIRE TO HELP THE HAVE-NOTS. AFTER ALL, IT WAS THE HAVE-NOTS THAT BESTOWED ON HIM THE CELEBRITY, FAME, AND FORTUNE.

STEP 6

I don't agree, you see, I don't really view communism as a bad thing.

—Whoopi Goldberg

HANDLING TIPS

- *Level One (couch commando)*—Hit 'em where it hurts—their wallet. When their latest romantic comedy comes out on video, opt for a movie that doesn't star someone who just compared the United States to Nazi Germany.
- *Level Two (fairly concerned citizen)*—Visit the local theater showing their latest movie and hand out flyers listing choice political statements made by the actor in question.
- *Level Three (ProtestWarrior)*—During a protest, confront them with your favorite PW sign ("Hollywood Activist" recommended) and include their guest speaker rants as background for your exposé video.

BUT HOW LONG WILL THE RIDE LAST? THIS IS HIS OPPORTUNITY TO DO SOMETHING MEANINGFUL AND LASTING. AND OF COURSE, THIS WILL HELP MAINTAIN THE ARBITRARY ADORATION OF THE MASSES. HE HAS BEEN GIVEN SO MUCH WHILE OTHERS HAVE NOTHING. SO HE BEGINS TO MAKE PUBLIC STATEMENTS EXPRESSING HIS CONCERN. WHY SHOULDN'T EVERYONE HAVE FREE HEALTH CARE, A LIVABLE WAGE, OR A HOME OF THEIR OWN? AFTER ALL, TO OUR ACTOR, THE ACCUMULATION OF WEALTH IS ARBITRARY. SO WHY SHOULDN'T THOSE WHO GOT LUCKY BE WILLING TO PAY WHATEVER TAX IS NECESSARY TO SUPPORT HIS SOCIALIST UTOPIA?

STEP 7

BLACKTIVISTS

CHAPTER 6

BLACKTIVISTS

Blacktivist: An angry, self-righteous protester who is true to his roots and demands equal justice for his people and an end to society's institutionalized racism. And, oh yeah, he's black.

IDENTIFYING CHARACTERISTICS

Blacktivists will typically wear African attire. These colorful duds are not actually made in Africa but are vaguely styled on African designs. The purpose of this fashion choice is to express their rejection of assimilation into American culture and to help avoid committing the cardinal sin of Blacktivists worldwide: *forgetting one's roots*. Blacktivist hairstyles can vary from shaved head to modified "afro" to full "afro" to cornrows to dreadlocks (often worn by Rastafarian Blacktivists). Other Blacktivists wear suits and ties, in the style of the Nation of Islam, usually separating themselves from the Afrocentric Blacktivists. These well-suited Blacktivists travel in flocks, do not smile, and do not talk, except when warning people to stay away.

Sometimes Blacktivists will carry incense, or wear T-shirts with images of Malcolm X or other black leaders. Signage typically carries messages accusing America of having the world's worst record on race relations, oppression, exploitation of minorities worldwide, and their favorite subject: "social justice." The icon of Blacktivist angst is Mumia

Abu-Jamal, a cabdriver and "apprentice in revolutionary journalism" for the Black Panthers, who was found guilty and sentenced to death for the murder of police officer Daniel Faulkner in 1981 (see Poster Boy). This cop killer and his supporters assert his innocence regardless of the overwhelming evidence supporting the guilty verdict, and an amateur observer can simply spot Mumia's picture or the phrase "Free Mumia!" on a sign to easily identify a Blacktivist.

Blacktivists exhibit a defiant, angry attitude, as they are only too aware of the pervasive racism that constantly surrounds them. Even if the racism isn't there, it really is there, as the racists are not even conscious of being the racists that they are. This concept of "unconscious" racism is what makes it possible for Blacktivists to thrive in the most racially harmonious country on the planet. Although it's technically possible for the oxymoronic "white Blacktivists" (known as "Whacktivists" in some circles) to exist, the self-loathing and guilt required to sustain such an existence are beyond what most are capable of handling. Even if the white Blacktivist is adamant about the racism pervading American society, these "Whacktivists" are rejected as annoying poseurs by their genuine counterparts.

THE ORIGIN OF THE SPECIES

The Blacktivist has seen the most radical transformation than any other protest species. Some experts suggest that the predecessors of the modern Blacktivists ought to be categorized as a separate species altogether (the name "honorable Blacktivist" has been suggested). This "honorable Blacktivist" incarnation has a long history of remarkable and heroic figures. Civil War–era honorable Blacktivists like Frederick Douglass (a former slave who literally freed himself from bondage) passionately fought against the evils of slavery and contributed enormously to the intellectual edifice that precipitated its eventual eradication. Intellectual giants and visionaries like Booker T. Washington paved the way for the newly freed black population, illustrating that the virtues of self-reliance and industriousness are inextricably linked to success in a free society. These self-made freedom fighters understood clearly the supreme values of life, liberty, and the pursuit of happiness promised by the Constitution, and their passion and intellect galvanized a revolution of universal freedom beyond what the Founding Fathers had even imagined.

Once the basic right of the freedom to do and say as you please was won with the passage of the Thirteenth Amendment's abolishing slavery, black suffrage became the next battleground. Although the Fifteenth Amendment was ratified in 1870, blacks were routinely disenfranchised by such insidious methods as poll taxes, intimidation, electoral fraud, literacy tests, and restrictive voting registration. It wasn't until the passage of the National Voting Rights Act of 1965 that blacks were federally guaranteed unfettered access to the voting process.

It wasn't until the issue of segregation that the Blacktivist species took a strange detour from the principles that had guided its forefathers. This new breed of Blacktivist no longer pursued equality before the law and the deinstitutionalization of discrimination. The Democratic Party, the previously proslavery party advocating the special rights of white people, was now for the special rights of black people. And black Americans were won over en masse to the Democratic platform, demanding *equality of results.* This was illustrated in the Civil Rights Act of 1964, which, although it outlawed voter disenfranchisement, desegregated public schools, and outlawed discrimination by government agencies, also outlawed discrimination in the private sector, where employers would have to answer to EEOC and would potentially face lawsuits if any job applicant felt passed up for any reason other than merit. This blatant violation of property rights and freedom of association was regarded as a necessary step by leaders like Martin Luther King, who said, "A society that has done something special against the Negro for hundreds of years must now do something special for him." This paradigm shift from preferential treatment of whites to preferential treatment of blacks was already in motion with Martin Luther King but really gained momentum with his most famous protégé, Jesse Jackson. Under this new doctrine, Blacktivists like Jesse Jackson and Al Sharpton set up large operations to "advise" companies and political bodies on their political correctness—vis-à-vis civil rights—and began charging hefty fees for their services. This new "equality of results" paradigm naturally led to the demand for race quotas, as any business that didn't reflect the public's racial mix, it could now be argued, was in violation of antidiscrimination laws. After being exposed to the corrosive gas of liberalism for decades, a new age of entitlement swept across black America, all but destroying the progress made by honorable Blacktivists.

Another bizarre departure from the Blacktivists of yore was the Nation of Islam variant of militant black separatism, tailor-made to confront the white world with its own unique prejudice. This strain's leadership, Louis Farrakhan and Malcolm X, rejected the notion of racial harmony outright and pushed for the segregation of blacks from whites, often exhibiting a proclivity to racism by condemning whites as inherently evil.

BEHAVIOR

Blacktivists project a defiant, separatist attitude, even toward liberal protesters who profess to share their political beliefs. This has to do with the Blacktivists' subconscious resentment of white leftists, who imply black inferiority with their assertion that blacks need special help and quotas in order to succeed. Blacktivists also subconsciously believe that whites can't help being the racists that they are, so better to stay away. You can observe Blacktivists segregating themselves from other protesters, and often accusing protest organizers of racist motivations for whatever it is they are doing, whether it's protesting the economy, carrying signs, or handing out water.

Blacktivists can also be surly around other Blacktivists. The afro-hair-styled dashiki-dressed city council Blacktivist is not going to be comfortable around the silver-suited Farrakhan Blacktivist, who is not going to be comfortable around the hip-hop Blacktivist, and so on. Blacktivists are very territorial, and each subspecies can behave in different ways. The middle-class Blacktivist is normally friendly and smiling and mixes with sympathetic whites. The Farrakhan follower is strangely aloof from everything in the white world, including its legal system, while the rap star is somewhere in the middle, using his music

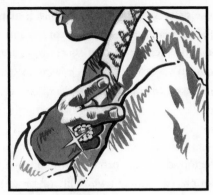

Figure 6.1: "Peace out"

to express the feelings and the experiences of the black community—the drugs, the violence, the badonkadonk—while acknowledging the adulation (and pocketing the dollars) of white music-buying fans. The only thing all Blacktivists agree on is the disease of racism—everyone's got it but them.

Blacktivists are very careful not to do anything that might cause them to be perceived as sellouts by other Blacktivists, and if they must watch *Friends* or listen to Steely Dan, they usually do so in private. Speaking out against the thuggery championed in rap music is strictly forbidden and can cost the violating Blacktivist all his street cred. A large vocabulary, good grades, infrequent use of "peace out" (see Figure 6.1), and a high-paying job in the private sector are all cause for suspicion, and voting Republican is immediate grounds for eternal banishment.

Some Blacktivists, especially Blacktivist historians, are very loquacious. They will talk at length about how black people in Egypt first invented things like gunpowder, cancer cures, and rocket ships, and how this incredible history has been twisted or hidden by the white man. While focusing on the pure evil of white slave traders transporting blacks from Africa, they de-emphasize or ignore completely the fact that the slave market was quite active in Africa before the arrival of the white man. In fact, the slave trade is still being conducted to this day in parts of Africa by Africans. A great deal of this revisionist black history is dumbfounding—and totally untrue. But never point that out to a

Blacktivist, because denying the truth of the black man's preeminence in religion, the sciences, and civilization is completely racist. Don't be confused by the overtly racist speech of Blacktivists. Remember: When blacktivists use the "n" word or call their women "hoes," it is completely appropriate, even endearing.

HABITAT

Blacktivists can be found at most protests, where they usually seem uncomfortably out of place. Although white liberal protesters espouse the cause of integration, they have a really hard time mixing with Blacktivists during protests or away from protests. Liberal protesters, especially Peace Moms, will fight to the death to support the integration of public schools, while they send their children to private schools to avoid "drug problems." Of course, there are usually three or four future

---

BLACKTIVISTS

THEN

Fredrick Douglass
1818–1895

Booker T. Washington
1856–1915

The Blacktivist species was once an honorable and incorruptible breed.

Thrived on: self-education
Likely to shout: "Free at last!"
Guiding principles: self-reliance, accountability, respect for the sacred value of property rights and the free market, pursuit of color-blind society.

NOW

Louis Farrakhan
1933–

Jesse Jackson
1941–

Let's take a look at how far gone modern Blacktivists have become . . .

Thrives on: self-aggrandizement
Likely to shout: "Free health care!"
Guiding principles: handout-dependent, blameless, "equitable" redistribution of private property and distrust of the free market, preferential treatment based on skin color.

Blacktivists in each private school, just enough to prove how liberal the private schools are.

Blacktivists trying to keep it real often live in Compton, Harlem, Houston's Fourth Ward, or some other "black" neighborhood. Living in these neighborhoods gives Blacktivists instant street cred. Of course, the few successful Blacktivists live in great wealth and luxury, impressing their liberal white friends with stories of the streets, even if they only lived there long enough to avoid a drive-by shooting. Some can be spotted as the sole black representative on a school board or community group, but most Blacktivists live with the black community, naturally enough. Many run stores with the word "African" in them. Blacktivists can be found in abundance at any publicly funded festival or arts event, which must be "inclusive," meaning it must include some Blacktivists. Blacktivists appear as storytellers or illustrators, but sometimes they just hang around these events—a paid presence to assuage the guilt of white funders.

CALLS OR SLOGANS

FREE MUMIA!
Black Power
Jobs Not Bombs

SOUNDTRACK SELECTION

While white protesters march to the tune of Dylan Wannabes, Blacktivists cruise to the beats of hip-hop and rap with Kanye West (whose mother was a Black Panther), Jay-Z, 50 Cent, Lil' John, and the sounds of the dirty, dirty South. Recordings to listen for include: Anything produced by Death Row Records. Anything recorded by Ludacris, the DJ turned rap star turned movie star from Atlanta whose albums include *Chicken and Beer* and whose immortal lines include, "I got hoes in different area codes" and the line from a love song about traffic management, "Move, bitch, get out the way."

THE PARTY LINE / BETWEEN THE LINES

We want power to determine the destiny of our black and oppressed communities. We believe that if the American businessmen will not give full employment, then the technology and means of production should be taken from the businessmen. . . . We want an end to the robbery by the capitalists of our black and oppressed communities. . . . Forty acres and two mules were promised 100 years ago as restitution for slave labor and mass murder of Black people. We will accept the payment in currency which will be distributed to our many communities. . . . We believe that if the landlords will not give decent housing to our Black and oppressed communities, then housing and the land should be made into cooperatives so that the people in our communities, with government aid, can build and make decent housing for the people. . . . We want decent education for our people that exposes the true nature of this decadent American society. . . . We want completely free health care for all black and oppressed people. . . . We want an immediate end to all wars of aggression. . . . We want freedom for all black and oppressed people now held in U.S. federal, state, county, city and military prisons and jails. . . . We want land, bread, housing, education, clothing, justice, peace and people's community control of modern technology.

—The Black Panther Ten-Point Plan

IN THEIR OWN WORDS

I don't put anything past the United States government. I don't find it too far-fetched that they tried to displace all the black people out of New Orleans.

—Spike Lee concerning federal response
to the 2005 Hurricane Katrina disaster

The Germans murdered 6 million Jews. The American racist has taken part in the slaughter of over 50 million black people.

—Black Panther Party

The Honorable Elijah Muhammad told us of a giant Motherplane that is made like the universe, spheres within spheres. White people call them unidentified flying objects (UFOs) . . . I entered the small wheel and the pilot whom I still could not see, moved the craft out of the tunnel and took it up to a terrific height and maneuvered his craft that I might look down upon the Mother Wheel. I saw a city in the sky. With great speed it brought me back to earth and dropped me off near Washington.

> —Louis Farrakhan, explaining his vision of being
> swept into a UFO, which he claims was his entire
> inspiration for the "Million Man March"

White people are potential humans—they haven't evolved yet.

> —Louis Farrakhan

Now that nation called Israel, never has had any peace in forty years and she will never have any peace because there can never be any peace structured on injustice, thievery, lying and deceit and using the name of God to shield your dirty religion under His holy and righteous name.

> —Louis Farrakhan

Jesus was born in Bethlehem. Jesse Jackson was born in Greenville.

> —Jesse Jackson

I say to Jewish America: Get ready . . . knuckle up, put your boots on, because we're ready and the war is going down. . . . The real deal is this: Black youth do not want a relationship with the Jewish community or the mainstream white community or the foot-shuffling, head-bowing, knee-bobbing black community. . . . All you Jews can go straight to hell.

> —Quannell X, national youth minister for the Nation of Islam

In South Africa we'd call it Apartheid. In Nazi Germany we'd call it fascism. Here we call it conservatism. These people are attacking the poor.

> —Jesse Jackson

They call them terrorists, I call them freedom fighters. No one asks why they would do such a thing. Why would they do such a thing? What has driven them to this point?

> —Louis Farrakhan on Hezbollah

If they don't pay us reparations now, we're talking about scorched earth.

> —Charles Barron, New York City
> councilman, at a reparations rally

A handkerchief-head, chicken-and-biscuit-eating Uncle Tom.

> —Spike Lee on Clarence Thomas

Civil rights laws were not passed to protect the rights of white men and do not apply to them.

> —Mary Frances Berry, chairman,
> U.S. Commission on Civil Rights

The white man is our mortal enemy, and we cannot accept him. I will fight to see that vicious beast go down into the lake of fire prepared for him from the beginning, that he never rise again to give any innocent black man, woman or child the hell that he has delighted in pouring on us for 400 years.

> —Louis Farrakhan

I mean, if black people kill black people every day, why not have a week and kill white people? You understand what I'm saying? In other words, white people, this government and that mayor were well aware of the fact that black people were dying every day in Los Angeles under gang violence. So if you're a gang member and you would normally be killing somebody, why not kill a white person? Do you think that somebody thinks that white people are better, or above dying, when they would kill their own kind?

> —Sister Souljah

BEST OF BREED

- Cornell West (b. 1953)—West, who grew up admiring "the sincere black militancy of Malcolm X, the defiant rage of the Black Panther Party," is a Harvard and Princeton graduate whose Ph.D. dissertation was entitled *The Ethical Dimensions of Marxist Thought*. West worked as a teacher and director of the African-American Studies programs at Princeton, then at Harvard, then back to Princeton. In addition to producing hip-hop albums (such as *Sketches of My Culture*) and appearing in science-fiction films, West teaches and writes books explaining his views as a "non-Marxist socialist." West worked as an advisor to Al Sharpton's presidential campaign and is deeply concerned about the plight of chickens in the corporate clutches of KFC.

- Louis Farrakhan (b. 1933)—Farrakhan is the leader of the Nation of Islam, a church built on the teachings of Elijah Muhammad, who believed that Allah created blacks first, then an evil sorcerer created devils with light skin—the white race. Farrakhan got into a feud with Malcolm X and declared, "Such a man as Malcolm is worthy of death." On February 21, 1965, Malcolm X was murdered by three assailants, two of whom belonged to Farrakhan's Nation of Islam. Farrakhan admitted, "I may have been complicit in words that I spoke leading up to February 21." Farrakhan formed his own Nation of Islam in 1977 and backed Jesse Jackson's run for the U.S. presidency in 1984. When Farrakhan got angry with Jewish reporters on the campaign trail, he attacked Judaism as a "dirty religion" and warned the Jewish people, "If you harm this brother, I warn you in the name of Allah, that will be the last one you do harm." Farrakhan led the UFO-inspired Million Man March in 1995 to support family values and to decry "white supremacy."

- Tupac Shakur (1971–96)—Named for a Peruvian revolutionary who was dismembered by horses, Tupac lived and died the "thug life." Tupac liked to shoot automatic weapons into his floor, was arrested for allegedly shooting at cops, attacked the director of the film *Menace II Society* with a baseball bat, and made a fortune selling CDs like *Strictly 4 My N.I.G.G.A.Z*. The quintessential Blacktivist rapper,

Tupac's favorite fight move was to lie down and kick at his opponents. In 1994, he was shot in a New York recording studio four times but only slightly wounded. On September 7, 1996, Shakur attended a boxing match in Las Vegas. After the match, Shakur spotted Orlando "Baby Lane" Anderson, a member of the Southside Crips, in the MGM Grand lobby. Shakur rushed him and knocked Anderson down, and Shakur's entourage beat him. Later that night, Tupac was shot and killed in a drive-by while driving in rap producer Suge Knight's passenger seat.

- Al Sharpton (b. 1954)—Sharpton first began delivering sermons at age four and met Jesse Jackson while touring the country as an ordained child minister. He made a name for himself taking "cases" for clients who wanted media attention, including that of Tawana Brawley, a fifteen-year-old black girl who was found smeared with feces, lying in a garbage bag, her clothing torn and burned and with various slurs and epithets written on her body. Brawley claimed that she had been assaulted and raped by six white men, some of them police officers, on November 28, 1987. Sharpton helped turn the incident into a media sensation and identified New York prosecutor Steven Pagones as one of the men involved, despite the lack of any evidence. Tawana's story was problematic from the beginning. A rape exam had come back inconclusive, further examinations revealed that she had received no real injuries, testimony from her schoolmates also indicated that she had been at a local party during the time of her supposed abduction, and her ex-boyfriend told *Newsday* that she had admitted to him that the story was completely made up. A grand jury was convened, and after seven months of examining police and medical records, the jury determined that Brawley's assault was a hoax. Steven Pagones, whose career and marriage had been shattered, was awarded $345,000 in a defamation-of-character suit he brought against Sharpton and others. Sharpton refused to pay and had one of his friends pay the judgment money. Sharpton refuses to apologize to Pagones to this day. Sharpton was arrested more than twenty times and jailed five times for illegal protests that included stopping traffic on the Brooklyn-Queens Expressway and closing the Statue of Liberty. "White folks was in caves while we was building empires," Sharpton once declared. "We taught philosophy and astrology and mathematics before Socrates and them Greek homos ever got around to it."

- Spike Lee (b. 1957)—Shelton Jackson Lee, called Spike by his mom because he was such a tough kid, started making award-winning films in college and hasn't stopped since. His first film, *She's Gotta Have It* (1985), was a huge box-office hit, and his later films have dealt with everything from racial issues to sex. Lee urged kids to skip school to see his film *Malcolm X*, declared NASCAR a racist institution, characterized Mississippi senator Trent Lott as a "card-carrying member of the Ku Klux Klan," and claimed that violence in the United States could best be stopped by disbanding the National Rifle Association and shooting Charlton Heston with a .44 Bulldog. Spike later apologized—at least for the last remark.

- Jesse Jackson (b. 1941)—A former college football player and an outstanding preacher, Reverend Jesse Jackson worked alongside Martin Luther King, Jr., before becoming America's most embarrassing unofficial diplomat. Jackson negotiated a hostage release in Syria, hugged Yasser Arafat, telephoned the Taliban, and interviewed Saddam Hussein. As the force behind People United to Save Humanity (PUSH) and the National Rainbow Coalition, Jackson never saw a protest he didn't like and has never passed up an opportunity to sound off. While running for U.S. president in 1984, Jackson referred to Jews as "hymies" in an off-the-record breakfast and described New York City as "hymietown." In a more general observation, Jackson declared, "It's impossible for white folks to perceive reality." This from a man who once declared, "If you deal with text out of context, you have a pretext."

POSTER BOY

Mumia Abu-Jamal, born Wesley Cook, is the most celebrated and recognizable cause taken up by the Blacktivist movement and is currently on death row for the murder of police officer Daniel Faulkner. At 3:55 A.M., on December 9, 1981, Faulkner, a twenty-five-year-old

Philadelphia police officer, saw a light blue Volkswagen driving the wrong way on a one-way street. In view of a number of eyewitnesses, he pulled the Volkswagen over.

Faulkner exited his vehicle and approached the Volkswagen, which was being driven by Mumia's brother, William Cook. Faulkner asked William to exit his car, and while he momentarily looked away, several witnesses stated they saw William violently attack Faulkner. Faulkner responded by striking Cook with his flashlight and then turned Cook toward the car, attempting to subdue him.

Meanwhile, sitting in a cab across the street and watching the events unfold, was William's older brother, Wesley Cook (Mumia Abu-Jamal). According to witnesses, Mumia exited his taxi, ran toward Faulkner and William, and fired one shot into Faulkner's back. Before he fell to the sidewalk, Faulkner was able to draw his gun and fire one return shot, hitting Mumia's abdomen. While Faulkner lay helpless on his back, Mumia was seen by four witnesses standing over the officer firing bullets at his upper body. Still conscious, Faulkner began to roll from side to side as Mumia fired at him, causing him to miss his first several shots. Mumia then bent closer to Faulkner, putting the muzzle of his gun within inches of his face, and squeezed off the final fatal shot above Faulkner's eye, the bullet entering his brain and killing him instantly.

During Mumia's trial, the evidence was substantial: four eyewitnesses to the entire event, forensic and ballistic evidence clearly pointing to Mumia, and Mumia's disruptive behavior during the trial. After two days of jury deliberation, he was found guilty of first-degree murder and was sentenced to death.

Left-wing groups around the world now maintain that Mumia was not given a fair trial and demand either a new trial or Mumia's immediate release, many of them claiming that he was framed by a racist police department trying to silence the progressive "journalist." After being imprisoned, Mumia continued his Blacktivism and published his book *Live from Death Row*, filled with his "musings, memories, and prophecies" on life inside prison. Left-wing colleges enamored of this cop killer, including UC Santa Cruz, Evergreen State College, Antioch College, and Occidental College, have allowed him to give commencement speeches to their graduating classes. This blind support of such an obviously evil, cold-blooded killer leaves many observers of the Blacktivist species utterly bewildered. Believing in such utter nonsense helps leftists maintain their fantasy that America is still a bastion of racism, and that blacks continue to be targeted by a predominantly white racist police force. Black people provide an important function for white leftists, as they assuage their guilt and let them feel better about themselves. After all, what would leftists do if blacks didn't need their help anymore?

HANDLING TIPS

- *Level One (couch commando)*—Make a phone call to Jesse Jackson's Rainbow Push Coalition to complain about the NBA's discriminatory hiring practices and demand an immediate investigation.
- *Level Two (fairly concerned citizen)*—When you encounter a Blacktivist ranting about the racist Republican Party, remind him that in the House of Representatives vote for the 1964 Civil Rights Act, 80 percent of Republicans voted to pass the act, compared to only 62 percent of Democrats. Be sure to include that it was leading Democrats Albert Gore, Sr., and Robert Byrd (a former Klansman) who filibustered against the bill for fourteen hours before the final vote. However, Blacktivists' brains are hardwired to repel any information that clashes with their directive that the Democratic Party is the only thing standing between them and the reestablishment of the Jim Crow laws.
- *Level Three (ProtestWarrior)*—Take out an ad in your local university newspaper with the text from the sign on page 229.

HACKTIVISTS

CHAPTER 7

▯▯▯

HACKTIVISTS

Hacktivist: Anyone who manipulates a computer system without authorization (or their parents' permission) to promote a political ideology.

MOONBATS TARGET PROTEST WARRIOR

By Michelle Malkin
July 06, 2005 10:28 AM

How unhinged is the moonbat Left? This report from Protest Warrior, the terrific conservative counter-protest organization, is a must-read. The group's website was targeted by an anti-war loon who apparently conspired with a group of hackers to steal the credit card numbers of some 5,000 members. FBI and Secret Service were called in to investigate. Excerpt:

> In January 2005, Jeremy Hammond and the hacker group collectively known as the "Internet Liberation Front" gained illegal access to the ProtestWarrior server. Thousands of customer credit card numbers were then stolen for the purpose of making millions of dollars in donations to various leftwing organizations. In early February, ProtestWarrior discovered the illegal breach and the identity of the criminals responsible.

IDENTIFYING CHARACTERISTICS

The Hacktivist is the newest addition to the creatures you might find at a protest. In fact, there was no such species as Hacktivist during the

Vietnam era. It has only been the recent proliferation of computer systems that gave rise to this peculiar breed. And while the world goes through the growing pains of securing these systems, our Hacktivist friends exploit any and all vulnerabilities to promote their typically anticapitalist message.

An attribute that is strikingly obvious even to the amateur observer is that this species is exclusively male. Although there are some who assert that female Hacktivists can exist in rare circumstances, the specimens that have been offered to back these claims have since been exposed as mere "script kiddies" (see glossary on pages 97–98). Breeding is often a touchy subject among Hacktivists, given the insurmountable odds they face in securing a first date. As a consequence, Hacktivists are almost always found at the end of a branch in their family tree. Spotting a Hacktivist in the wild can be tricky, since they prefer to confine themselves to their bedroom, often working till the early hours of the morning (even on school nights).

Years of minimal exposure to sunlight leaves the Hacktivist pasty in complexion, which doesn't do much to liven his severely wanting ap-

Figure 7.1: Away from keyboard

pearance. Disheveled, unkempt hair is often brazenly displayed to maintain the brilliant mastermind aspect of the Hacktivist's self-image. T-shirts are the standard uniform, usually bearing some sort of embarrassingly arcane acronym or witty Linux command (see Figure 7.1).

A Hacktivist's laptop is considered his pride and joy, and he will carry it around in a fairly deluxe case. If the Hacktivist is cautious, he will also carry a flash drive to hold all of the sensitive data he is currently dabbling with, which can be quickly destroyed if the authorities come calling. A number of recorded and blank CDs and DVDs labeled with a permanent marker can be found in a laptop case, including at least one pirated copy of *The Matrix* DVD (this film is used as a sort of rudimentary moral justification for their criminal activities).

Windows OS

While attempting to observe a Hacktivist in the wild, a surefire way to blow your cover is to refer to Microsoft or to Windows in any tone other than one of abject loathing. To a Hacktivist, evil has never been so singularly personified as it has been in the form of Microsoft and its products. Although Hacktivists are agnostic or atheist by nature, many of them believe that the anti-Christ exists in the form of its software CEO. However, a pirated copy of the Windows OS is mandatory to test their exploits.

Username/Alias

The decision on what username or alias a Hacktivist will go by is not made lightly. In fact, this decision is made in the same deliberate manner a music band or a DJ picks a name. This is the moniker the Hacktivist will build his alter ego around, the username he fantasizes will one day be associated with a vandalized system. Striking the ideal delicate balance of enigma and strength is absolutely critical. An alphanumeric mix is preferred, as they resemble a digital code (replacing "O" with "0" and "E" with "3" is not uncommon). Example usernames: r00g3r, soulsyphon.

ORIGIN OF THE SPECIES

Ever since the first humanoid scratched a pictograph on a cave wall, people have been creating code to keep stuff secret. And as long as there have been secret codes, there have been hackers. Hackers broke the codes of the Mesopotamians, the Mayans, Julius Caesar, Mary Queen of Scots, and even Arthur Scherbius, inventor of the Enigma machine. In the United States, the term "hacker" once referred to individuals who creatively manipulated a complex system, like the Cal Tech students who hacked the cheer cards held up by Washington fans at the 1961 Rose Bowl so they spelled out the words "Cal Tech." Captain Crunch and other phone phreaks led relatively benign attacks on communication systems in the 1960s and 1970s. With the appearance of Kevin Mitnick and the other "dark-side" hackers in the 1980s, hackers morphed from clever pranksters to petty crooks. If Hacktivists didn't take themselves so seriously, they might be dangerous.

TIMELINE

1878—First malicious use of phone system by teenage boys leads to banning by U.S. communications authorities.

1971—John Draper (aka Captain Crunch) discovers that the whistle toy prize found in the Cap'n Crunch cereal box emits a tone (2600 Hz) giving a user access to the internal trunking mechanism of AT&T, allowing for free long-distance phone calls.

1973—Entrepreneurial students Steve Wozniak and Steve Jobs (future founders of Apple Computer) begin making and selling blue boxes (devices that emit 2600 Hz tone).

1982—Six Milwaukee teenage hackers break into sixty computer systems ranging from Los Alamos Laboratories to Manhattan's Memorial Sloan-Kettering Cancer Center before being arrested.

1984—Legion of Doom (LOD) formed. Ruled hacker underground until the 1990s, when internal political disputes and Secret Service crackdowns led to group's disintegration (they, too, couldn't beat Superman).

1995—Kevin Mitnick is arrested by the FBI for wire fraud and breaking into the company servers of Fujitsu, Motorola, Nokia, and Sun Microsystems.

2000—"I Love You" virus appears and makes its way around the globe, infecting personal computers in a most unlovely way, rapidly spreading by sending copies of itself to all contacts from the infected computer's address book.

2006—Jeremy Hammond, founder of Hacktivist breeding ground hackthissite.org and leader of the "Internet Liberation Front," is sentenced to two years in federal prison for breaking into ProtestWarrior's server and stealing thousands of credit card numbers from ProtestWarrior store customers.

Figure 7.2

BEHAVIOR

Much like their close relatives the Anarchists, Hacktivists go to desperate lengths to secure their anonymity, but for much more justifiable reasons. Since they prefer to work in secrecy, spotting a Hacktivist in the wild requires years of rigorous academic study, rendering a sighting by a novice virtually impossible. Many times, the "hacktivity" will take place while the Hacktivist has strategically surrounded himself with innocent computer geeks (see Figure 7.2).

A Hacktivist usually spends his time casing targets and building an arsenal of exploits in order to "root" a server (see glossary). To a Hacktivist, "rooting a box" for the first time is akin to a bar mitzvah, a ceremony signifying the departure from their neophyte status where they are given props for their "mad skillz." The most typical targets are conservative-leaning websites, or if the hacker is feeling overly confident, defense-related government sites. A typical attack will usually consist of some sort of defacement or worse.

Today we are releasing a list of delegates to the 2004 Republican National Convention. This list includes the names, addresses, phone numbers, and e-mail addresses of RNC delegates in addition to what hotel each one is staying at during their invasion of New York City. Our objective is to supply anti-RNC groups with data on the delegates to use in whatever way they see fit.

—Indymedia Release, August 19, 2004, days before the Republican National Convention commenced in New York City

On March 17, 2005, nine Chicago FBI agents raided and seized all electronic equipment in Jeremy Hammond's apartment. Facing intimidation from both the FBI and the Secret Service, he is being accused of hacking into right-wing website ProtestWarrior.com. While the website had not been damaged and no credit cards were billed, the FBI is threatening to charge him with unauthorized access and credit card fraud totaling to millions of dollars in damages and up to thirty years in federal prison for a crime that hasn't even happened.

—Indymedia Release, July 13, 2005

IRC–Internet Relay Chat

IRC is the Hacktivist's main form of communication and is the closest thing he will have to a social life. This is where he will get help, discuss personal issues, and generally hang out. Almost all hacking is done using IRC as a communication medium. This is also where he will hatch plans or gloat over successful attacks:

IRC log excerpt between Jeremy Hammond (Xec96) and two members of the "Internet Liberation Front" discussing their plans to hack the ProtestWarrior server—February 1, 2005

[11:16.31] <Xec96> we have a complete user / pass list for every HQ (ProtestWarrior) member. these u/ps also double as email or even paypal accounts for these users
[11:17.42] <Xec96> we were thinking a round of donations. every PW who has ever ordered anything off the site will be making an involuntary contribution to various humanitarian and charity groups like the ALCU, etc
[11:19.48] <Xec96> the full names / home addresses / phone numbers / cell phone numbers of every single member will be released
[11:20.03] <Xec96> all this data will be spread all over the internet hundreds of indymedia centers, underground rings of hackers etc
[11:21.07] <Xec96> all the memebrs will be harassed incessantly
[11:21.12] <Xec96> have personal details revealed
[11:21.25] <IceShaman> they cant be that big can they?
[11:21.43] <IceShaman> you think any agencies would bother trying to track us down?
[11:21.44] <Xec96> the last time was a simple deface
[11:21.53] <Xec96> I don't think they'll have the finances to really fuck us over
[11:21.58] <Xec96> not only will the box be completely cleared
[11:22.02] <archaios> they won't but some of their members might
[11:23.21] <Xec96> I want to read some of their personal email. To get more details of who else they are working with.
[11:23.38] <Xec96> It's speculated they work with the Israeli government
[11:24.24] <IceShaman> a 2bit organisation does NOT make thousands a month

```
[11:24.38] <Xec96> this isn't a 2bit organization. they're
well financed and organized.
[11:25.52] <IceShaman> will you deface?
[11:25.56] <Xec96> I'd rather fry the box, then deface
[11:26.47] <Xec96> I'm feeling pretty safe about this
```

Most Hacktivist IRC channels are open (hackthissite.org, pulltheplug. org), but most of the time the IRC channels where plans for criminal activity are discussed are closed (you need to be invited, or in our case, you infiltrate).

HABITAT

Given the nature of the Hacktivist and the fact that they spend most of their life online, there really is no geographical point of congregation. Hacktivists can live anywhere, as long as they have an Internet connection and incognizant parents.

CALLS OR SLOGANS

Exploit code not people!
Hack wisely—protest wildly!
Dismantle the copyright industry!

THE PARTY LINE

We are building an international movement to defend the rights of all people to self-determination from the ruling classes of nations worldwide. . . . If corporations and governments are out of line to-day, it's up to cowboys of the electronic age to turn over the system and put the people on top. Electronic civil disobedience, modern day Robin Hood, cyber activism, hacktivists . . . we present the usage of hacking skills as a means to fight for social justice.

—From hackthissite.org, June 2004

BETWEEN THE LINES / IN THEIR OWN WORDS

Send fake emails posing as your boss and announce raises for everybody. . . . F&#k with rich people. . . . Organize a local anti-capitalist collective to strike terror in the hearts of the bosses and rulers. . . . Steal corporate credit card lists and donate money to charities. . . . Heckle your boss and/or union bureaucrat whenever possible. . . . Participate in a riot. . . . Hack a corporate or government website and fill it with anti-capitalist messages. . . . Write "This is your death" on every piece of money you can. . . . Throw a brick through a major corporation's window.

—cover of *Hackthiszine* publication introducing the "Hacktivist Manifesto"

GLOSSARY

Rooting—Rooting is the act of illegally gaining the highest possible access (root access) to a system. With root access, the Hacktivist is able to do with the server as he pleases—including deleting the entire contents. Example: "I'm trying to *root* foxnews."

Exploit—A vulnerability found on a system.

Script kiddie—A pseudo-Hacktivist who consistently attempts to gain access to a system using prepackaged attacks or scripts. These exploit scripts are usually written by bona fide hackers. Script kiddies are looked down upon for extreme unoriginality and ineffectuality. If this species actually had a mating season, a script kiddie would be automatically disqualified. Openly calling a Hacktivist a script kiddie is extremely derogatory and will be taken as a challenge to "root" your system.

2600—A number that is universally associated with hacking, deriving from the fact that 2600 Hz was the frequency in hertz (cycles per second) that AT&T formerly put as a steady signal on any long-distance telephone line. Early hackers developed a device that generated a

2600 Hz tone on a line, making it possible to call anywhere in the world without anyone being charged.

skillz—Displaying proficiency with an illegitimate activity, commonly hacking.

HANDLING TIPS

- *Level One (couch commando)*—Make a phone call to parents informing them of their son's misdeeds—will result in Hacktivist being grounded (and computer access revoked) for up to two months.
- *Level Two (fairly concerned citizen)*—Introduce Hacktivist to a girl—will render all thoughts of hacktivism a colossal waste of time. This handling option is difficult to execute given that compatible mates for this species are probably nonexistent.
- *Level Three (ProtestWarrior)*—Infiltrate Hacktivist's inner circle, gather evidence of his crimes, turn it over to the FBI, and send Hacktivist directly to jail.

ANTI-WAR HACKER INDICTED

By Michelle Malkin
May 26, 2006 10:18 AM

Our friends at Protest Warrior send word that the anti-war punk who gained illegal access to the ProtestWarrior server, stealing thousands of credit card numbers in order to commit massive credit card fraud, has been indicted. Excerpt:

> "Between January and February 2005, defendant [Jeremy] HAMMOND accessed ProtestWarrior.com's server without authority on multiple occasions in an effort to obtain information not otherwise available to him or the general public, specifically credit card numbers, home addresses, and other identifying information of the members and customers of ProtestWarrior.com."
>
> The specific violation is of Title 18, US Code, Sections 1030 (a)(2)(c) and 2. Per our understanding of the law, Jeremy faces a possible fine and imprisonment for up to 5 years.

PROUD MARYS

CHAPTER 8

||||||||||||||||||||||||||||||||||||||||||||||||||||||||||||

PROUD MARYS

Proud Mary: A homosexual whose life centers on letting others know about his or her sexual orientation and fetishes.

IDENTIFYING CHARACTERISTICS

Proud Marys are the peacocks of liberal protests, always doing their best to make sure everyone watching knows their sexual preference. Most Proud Marys literally glitter with the brightest, shiniest, most fabulous outfits in the protest. Others sport unattractively studded leather wear, or other fanciful garb. Female Proud Marys, like the female peacock, tend to be much less extravagant than their male counterparts, but nonetheless are striking in their masculine attire. Even if they were not so outlandishly plumed, it would still be quite easy to spot Proud Marys at a protest, since they are normally the only people holding hands, embracing closely or kissing at a protest, overt sexual behavior being a key identifying characteristic of this species.

Proud Marys are at their most flamboyant when participating in gay pride parades and other all-gay events. Floats in the shape of genitalia, near-full nudity, drag queens, and transgender high jinks are standard fare. But almost every protest will have a contingent of Proud Marys, with signs and chants trying to link gay liberation with the liberation of other oppressed peoples and progressive causes.

At many demonstrations about international affairs, immigration, or other major political issues, one wonders, What are Proud Marys doing here? Why do Proud Marys believe that global warming is related to their sex life? And why would they rally against toppling Saddam's regime, whose antisodomy laws permitted the murder of homosexuals with impunity? Leftist ideology isn't served à la carte—it's a package deal.

THE ORIGIN OF THE SPECIES

Though gay rights advocacy groups, such as the Mattachine Society, existed throughout the 1950s, it wasn't until 1969 that the modern gay rights movement was ushered in. On June 28, police raided the Stonewall Inn, a well-known gay bar in Greenwich Village, ostensibly for operating without a liquor license. Many of the patrons resisted arrest, resulting in three days of riots, which have since been dubbed the Stonewall Riots.

The disco era of the 1970s brought gays into the mainstream and into contact with just about everything imaginable. The party paused with the AIDS crisis, which became the thrust of the new gay movement in the 1980s. Although AIDS was an epidemic primarily in the gay community, many gay rights groups campaigned to terrify heterosexuals into believing they were just as much at risk (the odds of contracting AIDS during heterosexual intercourse with someone in a non-high-risk group without a condom are one in 5 million). Another falsehood spread by gay advocacy groups was that 10 percent of the population was homosexual (1 to 2 percent is a more accurate number), causing male heterosexuals around the country to speculate which one of their buddies was in the closet. Such misinformation helped gay rights groups garner support from the mainstream.

Lesbian feminists took to the barricades to tear down male-dominated society by introducing women's studies, women's bookstores, women's health clinics, and women's basketball teams. Other brands of sexually liberated individuals, bisexual, transgender, even man-boy lovers, jumped onto the Proud Mary bandwagon, although some Proud Marys refused to associate with activists of other sexual persuasion, including straights.

BEHAVIOR

Proud Marys insist that society should ignore sexual orientation, while at the same time throwing their sexuality in everyone's face. While marching, they show their pride with a lot of hand holding and smooching, insisting that everyone just deal with their public displays of affection.

Proud Marys are bouncy, vivacious, and well dressed (if dressed at all). Proud Marys can be flamboyantly gay, dressing in tie dye, feathers, boas, or even cross-dressing as women—from Baptist church ladies to Marilyn Monroe. The more mature elements of the species take the nerd approach, wearing sandals with socks, shorts, and perhaps a Hawaiian shirt, or perhaps dowdy sport coats and ties. Older Proud Marys tend to resemble one another, especially if they are a couple, and display symptoms of bickering behavior much like old married couples everywhere.

Female Proud Marys behave in several different ways. Some wear well-tailored suits and fine jewelry, while others wear torn T-shirts, jeans, and sneakers. Again, it's a question of age and style. Younger female Proud Marys party more. Like their male counterparts, they tend to drink a lot, and usually are up to date on the latest pharmaceutical concoctions. Older female Proud Marys take a more mature approach to political activism, and, like their male counterparts, bicker with their partners about dishes, real estate, and the kids, and are second only to Islamothugs when it comes to lack of a sense of humor.

Gays and lesbians have much more complicated sex lives than the rest of us—and not just physically. As one can easily glean from a single episode of *Will and Grace*, intrigues, endless heartfelt discussions, constant breakups and makeups lead to a much more annoying world of relationships than those in the straight world.

HABITAT

The Castro District in San Francisco and Greenwich Village in New York are the most well-known habitats for the Proud Marys. Other hip urban gentrified neighborhoods often morph into gay neighborhoods because they are the only ones that can afford to live there.

Other habitats/neighborhoods include (according to Out & About, an online travel site):

Chelsea (New York)—"With its epicenter at 18th Street and Eighth Avenue (the corner and the eponymous restaurant), Chelsea is New York's visibly gayest neighborhood, typified by its legions of young muscle boys, pumped-up and proudly parodying (oops! we meant parading) their sexuality."

Chestnutz (Palm Springs, California)—"A 'clothing-tolerated' resort with complimentary full breakfast, pool, 15-man Jacuzzi, misting systems, a lush garden and a no-attitude environment. You can go nude anywhere on the property."

Fort Lauderdale (bear country)—"Fort Lauderdale is one of the 'Bear Capitals' of the country, boasting a heavy gay bear population as well as many bear and bear-friendly resorts," including Bill's Filling Station, which is "wall-to-wall fur until about 10 p.m. This [is a] modest bar (with gas station theme decor, including an old-fashioned gas pump and dozens of old vanity license plates that say things like 'Bearcub' or 'Paws4U')."

SIGNS AND SLOGANS

Silence=Death

The government has blood on its hands. One AIDS death every half hour.

SOUNDTRACK SELECTION

Isn't it about time that people stopped using clichés to describe gay tastes in music? No. Here is a list of artists whose music is simply divine.

k.d. lang
Billy Bragg
Judy Garland
Elton John
Barbra Streisand
Cher

REQUIRED READING AND VIEWING

"Asian Pacific American Lesbian, Gay, Bisexual & Transgender People: A
Community Portrait"—Published by the Policy Institute in 2005, this
is a "groundbreaking report" that confirms "that 82% of Asian Pacific
American LGBT people surveyed had experienced discrimination
based on their sexual orientation." APALGBT people unite!

Rent—The Pulitzer Prize and Tony award-winning musical, which first
opened in 1996, is a lighthearted rock opera romp through Lower
Manhattan with a group of poor young artists who are worried about
AIDS. The cast includes the recovering heroin addict musician Roger
David, who is HIV positive; Joanne Jefferson, the Harvard-educated
lesbian lawyer; and Maureen Johnson, a bisexual performance artist.
What a slice of reality.

Pink Flamingos (1972)—Billing itself as "one of the most vile, stupid and repulsive films ever made," *Pink Flamingoes* introduced the world to the auteur John Waters and the brilliance of the cross-dressing Divine. In one scene, a cast member has sex with a chicken, which dies and is subsequently eaten. And that is not the worst scene, by far.

TIMELINE

May 1, 1970—The Second Congress to Unite Women was disunited when Rita Mae Brown and others did a "zap"—turned out the lights, pulled a plug on the microphone, and shouted slogans in support of "lesbian feminism." Some called the group the "Lavender Menace."

1973—Proud Marys founded the National Gay and Lesbian Task Force (NGLTF), as the first national lesbian, gay, bisexual, and trans-gender civil rights and advocacy organization. The organization states that it "consistently raises the interconnections between homophobia, transphobia, biphobia, sexism, racism, and classism."

March 1987—AIDS Coalition to Unleash Power (ACT-UP) begins operations, launching actions to protest the lack of funds dedicated to AIDS research. Actions include "die-ins," painting outlines of bodies on the street, and wrapping buildings with red tape.

March 1988—Hundreds of AIDS activists block traffic into New York's financial district, leading to about one hundred arrests and a lot of late trading.

November 24, 2003—Proud Marys ask gays, lesbians, and their friends to spend the holidays talking about Bush's antigay politics with a holiday campaign entitled "Talk Turkey: Bring It Home for the Holidays."

May 17, 2004—Proud Marys herald the first day of legally marrying same-sex couples in Massachusetts with the statement, "This wonderful day would never have happened but for the more than four decades of struggle for equal rights by lesbian, gay, bisexual, and transgender people all across our nation."

September 24, 2004—The National Gay and Lesbian Task Force premiers a short film entitled *Bovine Love Amendment*, which satirizes right-wing opposition to gay marriage. The film is part of an online campaign entitled "United States of Gaymerica."

BEST OF BREED

- Barney Frank (b. 1940)—The most prominently gay member of the U.S. House of Representatives, where he has represented the Commonwealth of Massachusetts since 1981. The Harvard-educated lawyer got into trouble when one of his ex-employees was running a male prostitution business out of Frank's apartment.

- Larry Kramer (b. 1957)—A Yale graduate whose 1970 screenplay for *Women in Love* was nominated for an Oscar, Kramer wrote the novel *Faggots* (1978) and the play *The Normal Heart*, about AIDS. Three years later, Kramer founded Gay Men's Health Crisis in New York and became America's leading gay activist. Kramer founded ACT-UP, which demanded free medical care for everyone infected with HIV, and blamed gay promiscuity on the discrimination of the straight world.

- Adrienne Rich (b. 1929)—A Radcliffe-educated poet, Rich declared in the mid-1970s that she was going "to write directly and overtly as a woman," then later came out as an overt lesbian. In her 1976 book *Of Woman Born: Motherhood as Experience and Intuition*, Rich exposed the "natural" phenomenon of childbirth as a social construct of ideological conservatives and patriarchs.

- Rita Mae Brown (b. 1944)—This lesbian writer tried unsuccessfully to introduce lesbianism as an issue within the National Organization for Women in 1969, as if they needed her help. She then moved in with a group of women activists who called themselves the Furies, then split furiously within a year. Brown became a celebrity with the success of her novel *Rubyfruit Jungle* (1973). She spent two years as the girlfriend of Martina Navratilova, then moved to L.A. in the 1980s and got into movies. Over the years, her attitude changed from one of lesbian separatistism to pansexualism.

POSTER BOY OR POSTER GIRL

The Pulitzer Prize–winning playwright and prominent Proud Mary Tony Kushner (b. 1956) is best known for his play *Angels in America*, which deals with AIDS and other subjects, and is the author of many other works, including *Hydrotaphia*; *Caroline, or Change*; *Homebody/ Kabul*; and *The Dead and Dostoyevsky, in a War with Bush*, a playlet in which Laura Bush talks about Dostoyevsky and refers to her husband as "the Chimp," which was performed for the liberal fund-raising group MoveOn.org. A fan of the *Communist Manifesto* who believes that Marx should be redeemed "from the mess Stalinism made of Marx," Kushner is the Proud Mary poster boy for the *New York Times*. Not only has he been mentioned in the paper more than four hundred times since 1996, but his 2003 wedding to Mark Harris, the editor of *Entertainment Weekly*, was one of the first same-sex unions to be mentioned in the "Vows" column of the Sunday *Times*.

HANDLING TIPS

- *Level One (couch commando)*—If you see a procession of Proud Marys, ask one of them what he's so proud about besides great abs and a really low body mass index.
- *Level Two (fairly concerned citizen)*—Next time a Proud Mary is protesting on behalf of an Islamic theocratic tyrant such as Saddam Hussein, remind him that he is backing a regime that would likely have him exterminated on sight, especially if caught in those Manolos.
- *Level Three (ProtestWarrior)*—Show the Proud Marys that you've got spirit, too. If you're heterosexual, and you're damn proud of your sexuality, organize your own Straight Pride parade and note how many times you're denounced as a "homophobe."

GRANOLAS

STEEL SPIKE TO
SABOTAGE MILL

ENVIRO-FRIENDLY TP

MINDLESS RAMBLINGS FOR
NEXT WEEK'S POETRY SLAM

LOOSENED IN CASE
LOGGERS CALL BLUFF

100% HEMP

CHAPTER 9

||||||||||||||||||||||||||||||||||||||||||||||||||||

GRANOLAS

Granola: Hippie environmentalists who would rather save a blind salamander than a human being. Granolas are the Chicken Littles of the protest world, for whom the sky is always falling, or at least getting warmer.

DOMESTIC TERROR BURNS SAN DIEGO

Center for Consumer Freedom
7/4/2003

Three workers sleeping at a construction site were able to escape after the terrorist Earth Liberation Front (ELF) set fire early Friday morning to an unfinished, 200 unit condominium development near San Diego. Nearby residents were evacuated and returned home to find their window blinds had melted from the heat.

"If you build it—we will burn it—the E.L.F.'s are mad," read a twelve foot sign next to the arson site.

IDENTIFYING CHARACTERISTICS

Since most ethnic minority activists are too busy focusing on their own plight, the Granola species is mostly made up of college-educated Anglos and light-skinned Europeans. Every other aspect characterizing the Granola is tied to their perceived relationship with Mother Earth. From the clothes they wear to the food they eat to the music they listen to, it must be in harmony with Mother Nature. Granolas have a very distinct dress code. Female Granolas wear long, flowing, tattered, and patterned dresses, while males will typically sport a tie-dyed T-shirt and torn jeans. When possible, their clothing is made from 100 percent "Earth friendly" hemp. Sandals are mandatory, and the more vegan Granolas will make sure they are made of "pleather." Female Granolas are notorious for taking all-natural to the extreme by neglecting to shave their armpits and legs, much to the disappointment of their male counterparts. However, they also eschew undergarments, which adds interest for the observant ProtestWarrior, especially when the female Granolas are up in trees—which is often. Granolas emanate the very distinct scent of patchouli oil, which makes for effortless identification by the novice observer. Other than helping them find a mate, this pungent natural extract is quite effective in masking the smell of marijuana and urine and can be used as dreadlock hair conditioner to boot. Dreadlocked specimens will typically wear a bandana tied tightly around their forehead to keep (quite understandably) the nappy tendrils from touching their face.

You will rarely find a Granola marching with a protest sign, given the unforgivable amount of timber the construction of such a sign would require. Instead, you can observe them at a protest parked on a grassy knoll, as they prefer to commune with nature while playing the bongos or hacky sack. Those who do march will most likely be holding up a rather large Earth First! or Green Peace sign, or an Earth Day flag (NASA photograph of Earth on a blue background) or some other graphic glorifying their efforts to protect the planet from greedy capitalists.

The older, more seasoned Granolas often wear expensive hiking boots, backpacks, specially designed hats, and breathable shirts and use expensive carved walking sticks as they make their way slowly up some godforsaken trail. But whether they are sitting in trees or liberating chickens or pouring red paint on expensive clothing, Granolas are sure that everyone is on their side.

THE ORIGIN OF THE SPECIES

Rachel Carson's *Silent Spring* (1962) is often credited with launching the creation of the Granola species. In her book, Carson attacked the chemical industry, claiming it was spreading disinformation about the dangerous pesticides that were harming the environment. Even though her arguments were often specious and her claims were refuted by many in the scientific community, she managed to scare the public into a total panic. Thus was born the Granola tradition of scaring the public with baseless claims of environmental and health crises in order to garner media attention and steady donations.

April 22, 1970, was also a pivotal date in Granola development, when the University of Wisconsin's environmental teach-in decided to call it "Earth Day." With carefully coordinated support from environmental activist Senator Gaylord Nelson, the demonstration received national news coverage. This annual celebration gave Granolas across the country the opportunity to gather in the streets and denounce the raping of the planet. As many liberal protestors soon discovered, the environmental movement proved to be a powerfully effective, semi–socially acceptable way to denounce capitalism and technology. It would be quite awkward to openly denounce industrial and recreational developments such as medicinal research, energy production, computers, shopping malls, and ski resorts for the stated goal of returning mankind to the primitive state of a cave dweller (though some Granolas have had success without the need to mask their agenda). So instead they sell their technological antagonism as a safety concern and drum up fear to garner support for their agenda. The anti–nuclear power movement of the 1980s fed right into the environmental cause, and Granolas worldwide did their best to terrify the public (children in particular) that nuclear power would lead to severe ecological destruction, nuclear meltdowns, and genetic mutations. That nuclear energy releases much less radioactive waste than coal power and produces zero greenhouse gases and that modern nuclear energy plants are safer than ever are facts that do not interest Granolas.

Soon radical factions got bored with pickets and protests and

12. Match each object with its proper handling method:

Answer: 1b 2a 3d 4c

Figure 9.1: Excerpt from Earth Liberation Front training manual

sought a more "direct action" approach. Led by theoretical weirdos like Edward Abbey, Granolas eventually began to perform acts of "eco-terrorism" until by the twenty-first century, they had earned a reputation as the Hezbollah of liberal protesters. By the spring of 2001, *U.S. News & World Report* reported that "the E.L.F. and the Animal Liberation Front have been behind the majority of terrorist acts committed on U.S. soil over the past two years" (see Figure 9.1). ELF and ALF worked clandestinely while their more mainstream counterparts continued their tag-team campaign of ecological fearmongering and ecoterrorism. Granolas now take issue with logging, genetic engineering, home building, the automotive industry, energy production and distribution, and anything else involving technology more complex than a rock and a stick—unless it's a really sweet ten-speed bike imported from China.

BEHAVIOR

In their striving to get back to nature, Granolas have wandered as far away from the natural rhythm of the marketplace as possible. They will constantly seek out alternatives to mainstream products that most of us take for granted. Fruit must be organically grown and chickens must be "non–genetically engineered" and free range. Some take it to the next level and avoid eating anything that has a face. This lifestyle usually comes with a higher price tag, which Granolas are often willing to pay. And when it comes to transportation, it absolutely must be "eco-friendly." Solar-powered, electric-powered, wind-powered, or human-powered—anything, as long as it doesn't derive power from the dreaded internal combustion engine. These alternative-powered vehicles can get expensive, and some Granolas break down and opt for a hybrid. After all, if you're going to rape the planet, the least you can do is kiss her on the cheek first. Still others opt for the most cost savings and drive around in SUVs, blaming the oil companies for keeping the prices for alternative-powered vehicles artificially high.

Granolas recycle everything, even when the recycling process does more harm to the environment than simply throwing stuff away. Since Granolas' entire existence depends on constantly whipping up public panic over some imminent world crisis (population explosion, global warming, the rain forest, acid rain, or any other headline-grabber), they will often come to your home to collect donations in order to combat the current danger to the planet. In order to survive to the next crisis, Granolas must obey their golden rule—never look back—lest they have to admit to themselves and to everyone else that their alarming and ex-aggerated predictions were dead wrong, again.

Another common activity is tree spiking—a form of sabotage that involves hammering a metal rod into a tree trunk in order to "discour-age" logging. When loggers attempt to cut down a "spiked" tree and the metal saw blade hits the embedded spike, the blade breaks or shatters. The resulting shattered blade, now an explosion of shrapnel, can potentially injure or kill nearby loggers. Even though this Granola practice has come under heavy criticism from official Granola leadership and has since been declared a federal felony, many members of Earth First! and ELF still consider it a legitimate tactic in their battle to save trees from becoming paper, houses, and furniture.

HABITAT

Look for Granolas in trees. Yes, trees. Tree sitting has emerged as one of the most popular forms of Granola protest. This activity consists of Granolas' climbing up to the top of a tree and chaining themselves to a trunk, safe in the knowledge that a logger wouldn't cut down the tree if it would endanger a human life. Sometimes Granolas stay in the tree for days, truly becoming one with nature as they linger without a shower or any basic hygiene. Some Granolas go so far as to make a tree their home, as Julia Butterfly Hill did for 738 consecutive days (see Poster Girl). The next step up in Granola living accommodations is the communal tree house. Some tree houses can hold up to twelve Granolas and come fully equipped with easily accessible lock-on points for the inhabitants to chain themselves to, to thwart eviction attempts by the property owners. Some Granolas have formed "Tree Villages," with several tree dwellings connected by rope. These Ewokesque villages are the pinnacle in Granola luxury and are installed with composting toilets, solar/wind power communications, cargo lines to the ground and to other trees, individual rappel lines, and hydroponic sprout farms.

Granolas approve of beaver dams, wasps' nests, and gopher holes, but they oppose any type of structure that is built by humans. For this reason, many Granolas inhabit planning commissions, zoning boards, and other local political conclaves. Granolas are born with the innate ability to sit patiently through endless hours of meetings to get what they want. Many Granolas secretly enjoy the air-conditioning and cushy chairs provided for them by the construction industries they oppose.

Granolas can be spotted in the ocean on small inflatable boats trying to interfere with whalers and military personnel. Granolas can also easily be spotted in rivers and lakes, paddling around directionless in canoes, kayaks, or home-built rowboats, complaining about the motorized vehicles and the people in them who are actually enjoying themselves. Look for Granolas near wilderness areas. Of course, the wilderness that Granolas prefer is a wilderness maintained pristine and preserved by high taxes. The most hardcore Granolas can be found living with seals or bears. That is, until the bears get hungry.

While Granolas often claim solidarity with native peoples, they really don't like the natives very much. Why? Because natives have to kill animals to survive, and most natives would much rather ride in a car than hike anywhere, especially if they are carrying something heavy.

As long as there's a Whole Foods or an organic deli nearby and they can comfortably donate to their favorite environmentalist charities, Granolas will be content to live in a mostly urban habitat, with all the creature comforts afforded by civilization.

SIGNS AND SLOGANS

No compromise in defense of Mother Earth!
Keep America Beautiful . . . Burn a Billboard

SOUNDTRACK SELECTION

Granolas groove to the sounds of the natural environment, filtered through millions of dollars' worth of digital recording equipment, package design, and marketing push.

The Last of the Mohicans: Original Motion Picture Soundtrack
Songs of the humpback whale
Any jam session by Phish

THE PARTY LINE/BETWEEN THE LINES/
IN THEIR OWN WORDS

Economic sabotage is the only thing the earth-raping, animal-abusing scum will respond to.

—Earth Liberation Front declaration

The human appetite for animal flesh is a driving force behind virtually every major category of environmental damage now threatening the human future—deforestation, erosion, fresh water scarcity, air and water pollution, climate change, biodiversity loss, *social injustice,* the destabilization of communities, and the spread of disease.

—Editors, *World Watch,* July/August 2004

If they won't stop when you ask them nicely, they don't stop when you demonstrate to them what they're doing wrong, then they should be stopped using whatever means necessary.

—Jerry Vlasak, Animal Liberation Front
spokesperson, on *60 Minutes*

The primate trade routes from Mauritius to the UK used by animal research facilities are as revolting and unacceptable as the slave routes used to transport black slaves from Africa to America in the 19th century.

—*Bite Back* magazine, May 2006

Perhaps the mere idea of receiving a nasty missive will allow animal researchers to empathize with their victims for the first time in

Here's Alan, minding his own business at our very first protest crash. © 2007 Amil Kabil

Kfir gets in touch with his feminist side.

Now with more signs and a better plan of attack, ProtestWarrior is born.

Crashing San Francisco.

The profound intellectual discourse of the Left.

Anna was never the same after being stood
up at her high school prom.

"Where did I put that acid?"

Painted in blood?

Hillary Clinton sets up her booth.

This must be what the U.N. is like.

ProtestWarrior takes on the left in Washington.

"Must hold sign . . . must block truth . . ."

Nothing can stop ProtestWarrior Truth.

Kfir leads the ProtestWarriors in New York.

Jenny speaks up.

their lousy careers. I find it small wonder that the laboratories aren't all burning to the ground. If I had more guts, I'd light a match.

—Ingrid Newkirk, president and cofounder of PETA

Animal liberationists do not separate out the human animal, so there is no rational basis for saying that a human being has special rights. A rat is a pig is a dog is a boy.

—Ingrid Newkirk

To those people who say, "My father is alive because of animal experimentation," I say, "Yeah, well, good for you. This dog died so your father could live." Sorry, but I am just not behind that kind of trade-off.

—Bill Maher, comedian and PETA celebrity spokesman

REQUIRED READING

Carson, Rachel. *Silent Spring* (1962). In this book, the former Pennsylvania farm girl turned *New Yorker* writer helped launch the environmental movement by claiming that pesticides were found in all living things and were killing fish and wildlife and endangering people.

Ehrlich, Paul. *The Population Bomb* (1967). The author declares that the population of humans on earth is growing so rapidly that by the 1970s and 1980s, "hundreds of millions of people will starve to death" (unless the world heeds his calls for radical reform). None of his ridiculous predictions came true, of course, and amazingly, Harvard has allowed him to actually teach students in the Population Studies Department.

Abbey, Edward. *The Monkey Wrench Gang* (1975). The fictional account of four knuckleheads who commit acts of sabotage in a deeply symbolic yet pointless attempt to halt progress in the American Southwest. Environmentalist saboteurs have since been deeply inspired by this work of fiction. Let's hope they don't read *A Clockwork Orange*.

ECOTERROR TIMELINE

February 28, 1992—ALF member Rod Coronado firebombs an animal research laboratory at Michigan State University, destroying thirty-two years of research data.

Spring 1997—ELF members attack a luxury home in Niwot, Colorado, a mansion in Boulder, and a house under construction on Long Island. In a communiqué, ELF states, "We know that the real 'ecoterrorists' are the white male industrial and corporate elite. They must be stopped."

October 18, 1998—Earth Liberation Front attacks developers of the Vail, Colorado, ski resort, destroying a chair lift, a ski patrol center, and a restaurant worth $12 million. In a statement, ELF declares, "On behalf of the lynx, five buildings and four ski lifts at Vail were reduced to ashes on the night of Sunday, October 18. . . . Putting profits ahead of Colorado's wildlife will not be tolerated. This action is just a warning. We will be back if this greedy corporation . . . continues to trespass into wild and unroaded areas."

February 2001—Brian Cass, managing director of Huntingdon Life Sciences, an animal-testing research company in the United Kingdom, was brutally beaten to within an inch of his life by three pickax-handle-wielding assailants. Dave Blenkinsop, who had engaged in actions on behalf of the Animal Liberation Front in the past, was jailed for three years for the attack.

Spring 2001—ELF sets fire to an Oregon tree farm to protest genetic research on poplar trees.

August 1, 2003—ELF arsonists burned down a housing complex under construction in San Diego, destroying a five-story building and a hundred-foot-high crane, with losses estimated at $50 million. Six weeks later, ELF operatives set fire to three other homes under construction in the area.

RELATED SUBSPECIES

One of the most entertaining (and repulsive) subspecies of Granolas are PETAs (People for the Ethical Treatment of Animals). Founded in 1980 by Ingrid Newkirk and headquartered in Norfolk, Virginia, PETA has spawned an absurd generation of animal-hugging protesters whose philosophy is: "Animals are not ours to eat, wear, experiment on, or use for entertainment."

PETA has fought for the rights of orangutans, chimpanzees, chickens, and force-fed geese, even masterminding ten thousand demonstrations against Kentucky Fried Chicken, enlisting support from Paul McCartney, the Dalai Lama, and Al Sharpton. Other PETA campaigns have focused on getting the University of South Carolina to change its mascot from the gamecock, and on Ringling Brothers Circus.

The real circus has been PETA's publicity-grabbing ad campaigns, which include:

An ad campaign claiming that Jesus was a vegetarian and featuring a pig with the caption, "He Died for Your Sins."

Performances of the Lettuce Ladies and the Broccoli Boys, PETA models who appear in public, clad only in strategically placed vegetables.

The "I'd Rather Go Naked Than Wear Fur" campaign, in which celebrities and activists protest naked and expose their own fur, while opposing the wearing of animal fur.

The "Are Animals the New Slaves?" campaign, in which pictures of slaughtered cows and chained elephants were displayed next to pictures of black slaves and Indians.

The "Your Mommy Kills Animals" campaign, in which PETA distributed a pamphlet to children under the age of thirteen showing a Mommy slicing open a rabbit's stomach, and the "Your Daddy Kills Animals" campaign, in which PETA distributed a pamphlet to children under the age of thirteen showing a Daddy gutting a fish accompanied by the text, "Since your daddy is teaching you the wrong lessons about right and wrong, you should teach him fishing is killing. Until your daddy learns it's not fun to kill, keep your doggies and kitties away from him. He's so hooked on killing defenseless animals, they could be next."

BEST OF BREED

■ Peter Singer (b. 1946)—Currently a professor of bioethics at Princeton, Singer is considered the Granola's intellectual godfather. "The question is not, 'Can they reason?' Nor 'Can they talk?' " Singer writes in regard to the ethics of killing animals, "but, 'Can they suffer?'" His 1975 book *Animal Liberation* had a major influence on the animal rights Granolas, referring to animal experimentation as "speciesist," meaning it shows discrimination against inferior species. He also holds that the right to life is based on the ability to plan and anticipate one's future, and therefore euthanasia can be justified in certain special circumstances. However, when Singer's own mother began suffering from Alzheimer's disease and lost her "right to life," according to Singer's ethical system, he declined pushing for euthanization, stating, "I think this has made me see how the issues of someone with these kinds of problems are really very difficult." Singer's ethical system is unique, giving him the ability to consider bestiality as a "logical conclusion" to some of the arguments he has made regarding the relationship of humans to animals.

POSTER BOY

Rod Coronado—As an activist for ALF, spokesman for ELF, former crew member of the Sea Shepherd Conservation Society, and editorial member of the *Earth First!* journal, Rod lived and breathed ultraorthodox Granola doctrine. Rod began his illustrious career in ecoterror at the age of twenty, when he and another activist sank half of Iceland's whaling fleet and managed to cause $2 million in damage to their whaling station. This brazen act at such a young age instantly turned Rod into a rising star in the Granola-terror community. Many ecoterror ops later, Coronado was finally jailed in 1995 for an arson attack on research facilities at Michigan State University, destroying thirty-two years of research data. On December 13, 2005, he and codefendant Matthew Crozier were found guilty of felony conspiracy to interfere with or injure a government official, misdemeanor interference with or injury to a forest officer, and misdemeanor theft of government property. Coronado was sentenced on August 6, 2006, to eight months in prison and three years' supervised probation. After a decade of criminal behavior, in September 2006, Coronado finally began feeling what healthy humans like to call "remorse." Not quite enjoying the consequences of destroying other people's private property, he sent an open letter to supporters from his prison cell in Florence, Arizona, urging others in the earth and animal liberation movements to consider more "peaceful" methods.

POSTER GIRL

Julia Butterfly Hill is perhaps the most famous Tree Granola, living in a tree she called "Luna" between December 10, 1997, and December 18, 1999, for a grand total of 738 consecutive days, preventing loggers from cutting it down. Julia wasn't always a Granola. She became one immediately after she suffered a mild brain injury in a car crash a year before her tree stint—pure coincidence, of course. The lumber company that owned the tree agreed to preserve "Luna" in all her leafy splendor and all the trees within a three-acre buffer zone in exchange for Hill's promise to vacate the tree and fifty thousand dollars that Hill and other activists had raised during the two-year publicity stunt. Hill instantly became a celebrity in the Granola universe, was the subject of the documentary film *Butterfly* in 2000, and was featured in the documentary film *Tree-Sit: The Art of Resistance*. Even renowned Granola jamband Phish chimed in and wrote a song called "Kissed by Mist" about Julia.

Inspired by Hill, Hollywood Activists (see Chapter 5) Daryl Hannah and Joan Baez recently took up residence in a walnut tree at the South Central Community Garden in Los Angeles in May 2006. In accordance with the Granola doctrine of ignoring property rights, the tree-dwelling trespassers attempted to stop garden landowner Ralph

Horowitz from developing his own property. Why? Because working-class immigrants were using his property to "tend their crops," as if this has any legal relevance to what Mr. Horowitz is or isn't allowed to do with his land. In the end, the city of Los Angeles decided to enforce Horowitz's property rights, and on June 14, 2006, the police removed the activists from the property, cutting away branches to remove Daryl Hannah from the walnut tree she had been living in for three weeks and arrest her. Daryl eventually made it back to the comfort of her palace in Malibu and doesn't plan on opening her security gates so that the farmer immigrants can "tend their crops" on her sprawling property—such a disruption would make it difficult for Daryl to gather her daily thoughts for her online activist blog, dhlovelife.com.

HANDLING TIPS

- *Level One (couch commando)*—Take a moment to appreciate all the things animals make possible for us humans, like providing us with durable leather goods, tasty foods, safer chemicals, medical advances, and increasing our life expectancy by twenty-five years. And if animal rights activists boycott or harass a business you benefit from, make it a point to increase your patronage.
- *Level Two (fairly concerned citizen)*—When you see a flock of PETAs demonstrating in front of your favorite fast-food joint, ask them if they would like for you to get any of them something to eat as you walk in.
- *Level Three (ProtestWarrior)*—Take a jambox to a "Tree Village" and play a recording of a chain saw at full volume. Make sure you turn up the bass and, if possible, carry a chain saw with you for maximum effect.

PEACE MOMS

CELEBRITY SIGHTING ALERT
FROM FELLOW PEACE MOM

PETITION TO MANDATE
NEIGHBORHOOD RECYCLING PROGRAM

CHRONIC EXERCISE

CHAPTER 10

||||||||||||||||||||||||||||||||||||||||||||||||||||||||||||

PEACE MOMS

Peace Mom: A well-organized, well-caffeinated member of the suburban leisure class who has an overwhelming need to "make a difference."

IDENTIFYING CHARACTERISTICS

If you see a Democratic bumper sticker on a Mercedes, Jaguar, or Volvo, you can be almost certain that you are in the presence of a Peace Mom. This includes any sighting of a peace sign flag or even a Tibetan prayer flag (the farther away the issue is from their own lives, the more commitment you will see from Peace Moms). You will often find this specimen smiling a lot, kissing people on the cheek, and hugging indiscriminately. They are by far the best smelling of all the species.

Peace Moms are team players, as long as the team consist of one—themselves. And nothing improves their status in the eyes of the other Peace Moms more than having successful kids. But once the children have moved out, what's a Peace Mom to do? The skills learned at the PTA meetings and the neighborhood recycling drives help them with the natural transition to liberal protests—which makes Peace Moms one of the most dangerous species of liberal protester. Although they don't quite know what they're doing, they actually get things done. They are organized, well spoken, and usually sober until the postdemonstration glass of wine or three. With years of chauffeuring experience, Peace

Figure 10.1: Peace Mom on Board

Moms sometimes serve as the armored divisions of liberal protesters. They have dependable cars, Volvo station wagons, Subarus, even an SUV or two. "I know it uses a lot of gas, but I need the car for my work."

Peace Moms are clinically addicted to meetings and can be classified as aggressive "email hoes." The making and changing of schedules is a near-constant activity, since protests must fit in with other vital obligations—hair appointments, doctor appointments, dinner, lunch, and coffee dates with friends and enemies. Peace Moms feel most righteous when they spend hundreds of hours organizing events that raise amazingly small amounts of money.

They can always be found at the head of a protest procession, making sure everyone in the crowd acknowledges their hard-earned figure. Holding signs proclaiming their maternity and sprightly displays of their offspring are common and are very effective in getting them some much-craved TV coverage.

THE ORIGIN OF THE SPECIES

Former homemaker turned home complainer Betty Friedan (1921–2006) spawned Peace Moms with the publication of *The Feminine*

Mystique in 1963. While raising three kids and studying at the University of California and the Esalen Institute, the former Betty Naomi Goldstein wrote articles describing the joys of life as a homemaker until she was fired from a job for what she claims was taking a maternity leave. This action turned homemaker Betty into Betty the man-hating blowhard. Friedan was founder and first president of the National Organization for Women (NOW) in 1966. To her credit, Friedan fell from that position when she opposed the hardcore lesbian and radical fringe wing of the organization (calling it "the lavender menace") when they rejected the family unit as dysfunctional and oppressive.

NOW is still one of the Peace Moms' main organizations, with more than half a million members in 550 chapters across the United States. Friedan's biggest theoretical revelation in *The Feminine Mystique* was that all women suffered from "the problem that has no name." The problem now has a name—Peace Moms.

Friedan's writing launched the women's liberation movement, or the women's movement, or feminism, which in turn has evolved through various phases with spokeswomen from Germaine Greer to Gloria Steinem to Naomi Wolf. But whether it's third-wave feminism, women's liberation, women's studies, women's music, women's literature, or women's anything, the basic message remains the same—men bad, women good, and I'm the most attractive creature on the planet.

BEHAVIOR

Peace Mom boot camp typically entails making brownies for elementary school bake sales, selling homely Christmas wrapping at middle school fund-raisers, attending teacher conferences, hustling Girl Scout cookies, and attending hundreds of hours of sporting events with their kids. Then, as Betty Friedan first noted, Peace Moms begin to wonder, is that all there is to my life? That's when the real trouble begins.

After a Peace Mom graduates from being active in the home, then the PTA, and then community issues, it's time to move on to more ambitious territory. After paying their dues organizing Halloween and Christmas parties and the neighborhood recycling campaign, more formal training can begin. This usually entails involvement with a liberal organization such as Planned Parenthood, helping everyone get laid as perhaps a substitute for their own unfulfilled desires. Psychologically, some of the Peace Moms are returning to their college years, when they attended protests to unionize cafeteria workers, save trees on campus, or spit on "baby killers" returning from war. Usually Peace Moms begin participating in local protests, asked by one of their wilder friends, or to show their kids that at one point Mommy used to be "cool."

Often Peace Moms will claim they admire other women who have gone on to success in various fields. However, Peace Moms all suffer from the queen bee syndrome. And if they aren't the queen bee of any enterprise, they will plot and scheme to bring down their rivals. That's why there is usually not a group of Peace Moms at any one protest or any one event.

Money means little to Peace Moms because they have so much of it. Peace Moms quit work to raise their kids and complain about oppression by men—including their husbands (usually successful professionals), who pay the bills. Peace Moms may not know how the world works, but they do know how to work their small corner of it to get themselves the best hairdo, personal trainer, and café latte Frappuccino in the city. Peace Moms adore being adored, but they are usually too busy for sex, especially with someone who has to work for a living. However, it has been observed in the wild that the only other species a Peace Mom will be sexually attracted to is the Hollywood Activist.

Usually a Peace Mom will be active until the grandkids are born, at which point she will give up the world of politics and revert to homemaker, taking care of the grandchildren so that they, too, will reflect well on her. Of course, some women stay in the political arena and become Peace Grandmas, the gray-haired old ladies who sit in chairs and tell everyone about their grandkids for peace. After they have been grandmas for a while, they often wish to become sexy again and write come-hither tracts about the wonders of sex after eighty. Yes, it is a wonder.

HABITAT

Peace Moms usually inhabit upper-middle-class suburbs near college towns, or anywhere in California or the Northeast. They have well-kept homes but spend most of their lives in their cars, on their cell phones or on the Internet, where they shop for tennis wear between organizing protests against the evils of corporations.

Anything prefaced by "Women" is a good place to observe this species. Women's health club. Women's Soccer League. Or your neighborhood women's softball team. Especially women's sports teams, as Title IX was the clarion call of Peace Moms for years. And now women have much more opportunity than men to play sports in college, and play them badly.

CALLS OR SLOGANS

> Don't Cry: Resist
> Let the Children Grow
> End the Arms Race, Not the Human Race
> Not my son, not your son, not their sons.
> Don't Iron While the Strike Is Hot

SOUNDTRACK SELECTION

Joan Baez—The original women's protest voice and still going strong, Baez started her career in the coffeehouses in Cambridge and toured with Bob Dylan before he broke up with her. Never sold many records but has never avoided a protesting microphone.

The Dixie Chicks—This Texas trio made headlines at a concert in England when they said, "We're ashamed the president of the United States is from Texas." The Chicks foot-in-mouth disease did not slow the sales of their albums, which include lighthearted ditties like "Goodbye Earl," a song about killing one's husband.

THE PARTY LINE / BETWEEN THE LINES

The Party Line: "When the Jolly Green Giant is on a rampage, many lesser plants and animals get trampled underfoot" (Margaret Atwood, Canadian writer who studied at Radcliffe).

Between the Lines: We Canadian women know how to run a country.

The Party Line: The stated goal of the National Organization for Women is "to take action to bring women into full participation in the mainstream of American society now, exercising all the privileges and responsibilities thereof in truly equal partnership with men."

Between the Lines: It's my husband's fault.

The Party Line: Women deserve "the choice to do whatever we want with our faces and bodies without being punished by an ideology that is using attitudes, economic pressure, and even legal judgments regarding women's appearance to undermine us psychologically and politically" (Naomi Wolf in *The Beauty Myth* [1991]).

Between the Lines: Do you know where I can get a good pedicure?

REQUIRED READING

Greer, Germaine. *The Female Eunuch* (1970). Ms. Greer discusses "the castration of women."

Dworkin, Andrea. *Woman Hating* (1974). Ms. Dworkin discusses footbinding, genital mutilation, pornography, and fairy tales.

Dworkin, Andrea. *Intercourse* (1987). Ms. Dworkin describes the sex act as the "formal expression of men's contempt for women."

Faludi, Susan. *Backlash: The Undeclared War Against American Women* (1991).

Perhaps the most revealing title in the entire women's literary genre is the classic *Our Bodies, Our Selves* (Boston Women's Health Book Collective).

POSTER GIRL

Cindy Lee Miller Sheehan (b. 1957) was a lifelong Democrat and a Peace Mom in Berkeley, California, until her son Casey Sheehan was killed in Iraq. In June 2004, Sheehan met with President Bush accompanied by other military families and explained to the press, "I know he's sorry and feels some pain for our loss," and that the visit had given her back the "gift of happiness." Then, in a matter of months, the loyal and sorrowing Peace Mom transformed into "Peace Mom." She described her meeting with the president as "one of the most disgusting experiences I've ever had and it took me almost a year to even talk about it."

The transformed Ms. Sheehan founded Gold Star Families for Peace, and in the fall and winter of 2005 helped organize a Bring Them Home Now Tour, along with Veterans for Peace, Iraq Veterans Against the War, and Military Families Speak Out. Sheehan was the darling of the media until she spun totally off the tracks. She called John McCain a warmonger and protested Hillary Clinton's stance on the war. She traveled to Venezuela, joined ten thousand other liberal protesters at an antiglobalization rally, and stood on a podium with Hugo Chavez, where she declared, "I admire President Chavez for his strength to resist the United States."

At the 2006 State of the Union Address, Sheehan, who was in the audience at the invitation of Representative Lynn Woolsey (D.-Calif.), stripped down to a T-shirt that proudly read "2,245 dead. How Many More?" She was handcuffed and removed from the gallery before the president began to speak. A few months before the unfortunate underwear protest by "the Rosa Parks of the antiwar movement," Sheehan's husband of twenty-eight years filed for divorce, without listing any reasons. Did he really have to?

HANDLING TIPS

- *Level One (couch commando)*—Compliment a Peace Mom and ask her about her workout regimen. You will have to endure a half-hour talk at the minimum. However, by the end she will have all but forgotten about whatever protest is going on.

- *Level Two (fairly concerned citizen)*—Tell a Peace Mom that her mascara is running. She will immediately disappear from the protest and head home for a thorough makeup reapplication.
- *Level Three (ProtestWarrior)*—Interview her about the evils of capitalism and follow up with asking her where her husband works.

SELF-HATING VETS

CHAPTER 11

SELF-HATING VETS

Self-Hating Vet: A confused former military man or woman who, through factors way beyond anyone's control, has traded military common sense for the common insanity of the left.

IDENTIFYING CHARACTERISTICS

Every protest has a handful of Self-Hating Vets in attendance. Their appearance is unique enough that even the most novice observer should have no trouble spotting one in the wild. A Self-Hating Vet almost always sports long hair sprouting over a sweaty headband (camouflage is typical). An unbuttoned (no choice due to pot belly) camouflage fatigue jacket with the sleeves cut off is considered mandatory, and he will typically be carrying an army-issue haversack toting most of his possessions (Figure 11.1).

THE ORIGIN OF THE SPECIES

The Self-Hating Vet evolved from a combination of two powerful forces—the conflict of the 1960s in Southeast Asia and the herbal essence of the 1960s on American college campuses. Having served in Saigon and Orange County, the Self-Hating Vet left behind all loyalty to the armed forces, lured away by the powerful scent of pot and the

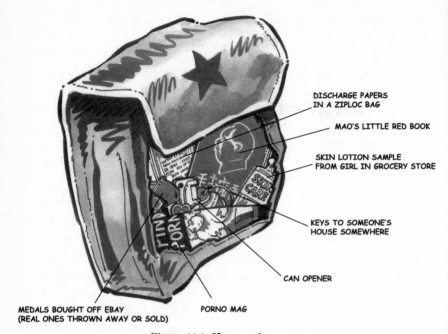

DISCHARGE PAPERS
IN A ZIPLOC BAG

MAO'S LITTLE RED BOOK

SKIN LOTION SAMPLE
FROM GIRL IN GROCERY STORE

KEYS TO SOMEONE'S
HOUSE SOMEWHERE

CAN OPENER

MEDALS BOUGHT OFF EBAY   PORNO MAG
(REAL ONES THROWN AWAY OR SOLD)

Figure 11.1: Haversack contents

endless supply of nubile female protesters of the 1960s. With aviator shades, headband, fatigues, and long hair, the Self-Hating Vet kept busy with the liberals and their liberal use of mind-altering substances. While many veterans joined the American Legion or the Vietnam Veterans of America, the Self-Hating Vet continued to take to the streets even after the end of the Vietnam War in 1975. But as the years went by, the Self-Hating Vet sort of lost track of what the protest was all about—nuclear energy? global warming? trade? the World Series?—and found himself outside the American mainstream, marching along with the hope of scoring some pot, some chicks, or maybe a dry place to sleep. He still has a voice, or what's left of a voice after spending so many days at busy intersections, panhandling and whining about war criminals—the servicemen and -women who served with him in the military and continued to fight for their country.

BEHAVIOR

While the behavior of some veterans has been seriously affected by post-traumatic stress disorder, the most traumatic stress faced by the Self-Hating Vet is answering the question, Where did I put my lighter? On the whole, Self-Hating Vets are the most mellow and easygoing species—almost to the point of catatonic. Occasionally, when they start partying with a group of young protesters, they have a tendency to spin out into a nether world of convoluted observations on everything from international foreign policy to carburetors.

Self-Hating Vets have trouble holding jobs. This is not because of Agent Orange, but because they may spend three or four hours every morning recovering from an acid trip and searching for hidden cameras in their living rooms or sweeping the apartment for bugged phone lines. Many Self-Hating Vets are attracted to government work—like working for the post office, or for an animal control unit, or for the county road service, or for the veterans' services administration. They can be obstinate at times, and are sure they know the best way to do things, whether it's fixing a cabinet or tailing CIA operatives.

Self-Hating Vets usually drive old cars, oftentimes vans. This is primarily because they don't make much money and also because it reflects their aging hippie lifestyle. Self-Hating Vets are often the most long-winded of protesters. They will often tell of their psychedelic experiences, mixing tales of their military life with tales from American Indian mythology or random episodes of *Star Trek*. One thing is almost universal: Wherever the Self-Hating Vet is working or just hanging out, he will always be willing to tell anyone who will listen just how it really was in Nam.

HABITAT

Self-Hating Vets can be found at the center of most protests, though sometimes they don't know which protest they are attending. You may also observe them at your local public library researching obscure points of international diplomacy, physics, or sexually transmitted diseases.

Some of the most successful Self-Hating Vets run Volkswagen repair shops or live near the coasts of Mexico or Southeast Asia, where their vast hair, vast weight, and erratic tempers make them perfectly suited to work as bouncers in beachfront bars.

Self-Hating Vets in the United States can often be found smoking in the front of office buildings. Taverns are also a common habitat for Self-Hating Vets, as they tend to drink more than other protester species, and there they engage in long-winded political discussions with bartenders or neon Miller beer signs. Look for Self-Hating Vets near college campuses, conversing intently with female College Students (see Chapter 4) wearing low-cut jeans and tight T-shirts. This is a fleeting habitat, as most young women only allow for a five-minute discussion, just enough so that they feel comfortable that they have put in their obligatory time "for the cause."

And of course, some Self-Hating Vets can be found under bridges or roadways, in public parks or public lavatories, and in public plazas or at free outdoor concerts, anywhere where there is the faint scent of marijuana.

SIGNS AND SLOGANS

Ho, Ho, Ho Chi Minh
That's the way we did it in Nam.
Hey Hey LBJ, How Many Kids Did You Kill Today?

VVAW

From the VVAW website: "We took the U.S. Military Assistance Command (MACV) patch as our own, replacing the sword with the upside-down rifle with helmet, the international symbol of soldiers killed in action. This was done to expose the lies and hypocrisy of U.S. aggression in Vietnam as well as its cost in human lives. As with all the propaganda put out by the government to justify U.S. intervention in Indochina, the MACV insignia also put forward lies. . . . Our insignia has come to represent veterans fighting against new 'adventures' like

the Vietnam War, while at the same time fighting for a decent way of life for veterans and their families."

SOUNDTRACK SELECTION

Self-Hating Vets stopped listening to new music in 1975. Here are a few classic rock Self-Hating Vet hits.

> Jim Morrison and The Doors: "Light My Fire"
> Jimi Hendrix: "Star-Spangled Banner"
> Janis Joplin: "Piece of My Heart"

THE PARTY LINE

> "We believe that service to our country and communities did not end when we were discharged. We remain committed to the struggle for peace and for social and economic justice for all people. We will continue to oppose senseless military adventures and to teach the real lessons of the Vietnam War" (VVAW mission statement from their webpage).

BETWEEN THE LINES

> We continue to support any senseless cause we can, as long as they are in opposition to the U.S. military, and as long as they don't interfere with the benefits we continue to receive from the U.S. military.

REQUIRED READING

Kerry, John, and Vietnam Veterans Against the War. *The New Soldier* (1971).

O'Neill, John, and Jerome Corsi. *Unfit for Command: Swift Boat Veterans Speak Out Against John Kerry* (2004).

Nicosia, Gerald. *Home to War: A History of the Vietnam Veterans' Movement* (2001).

"Vietnam, A View from the Walls" (http://www.greenwych.ca/vietnam. htm).

REQUIRED VIEWING

Coming Home (1971), also known as Going Down—every Self-Hating Vet's dream—oral sex with Jane Fonda.

TIMELINE

June 1967—Six Self-Hating Vets founded the Veterans for Peace movement after marching in protest of the Vietnam War at an April 15, 1967, rally in New York City known as the Spring Mobilization to End the War.

Labor Day 1970—Over 150 Self-Hating Vets took part in a protest called Operation RAW ("Rapid American Withdrawal"). As part of the protest, the Self-Hating Vets marched to Valley Forge State Park where they re-enacted search-and-destroy missions in a lame attempt at what was referred to as "guerilla theater." The only trouble with the theatrical protest was that the members of the Youth International Party, who had agreed to play the Vietcong, changed their minds at the last minute because they said being blindfolded during the performance was a "bore."

April 21, 1971—Fifty Self-Hating Vets tried to surrender at the Pentagon and declare themselves war criminals. Pentagon officials refused to receive the group, but Senator Ted Kennedy welcomed them and spoke with them for much of the day. On April 22, a young John Kerry, acting as a spokesperson for the Vietnam Veterans Against the War organization, testified on behalf of the protesting Self-Hating Vets in front of the Senate Foreign Relations Committee. These high jinks were followed by yet another Self-Hating Vet display as eight hundred Self-Hating Vets tossed away their discharge papers and military decorations from the steps of the U.S. Capitol Building.

August 13, 1971—According to FBI files, Joseph Urgo, the second vice president of VVAW, traveled to Hanoi and met with North Vietnamese officials. Among other things, Urgo reportedly proposed sending tapes from the United States to broadcast over Radio Hanoi to convince U.S. servicemen to stop fighting.

December 1971—Fifteen Self-Hating Vets occupied the Statue of Liberty for two days by barricading themselves in the statue. In a related incident, less efficient Self-Hating Vets took command of the Betsy Ross house in Philadelphia for forty-five minutes.

Since the end of the Vietnam War in 1975, Self-Hating Vets have dedicated themselves to working for peace and social justice, which means they really haven't been doing much except hanging around. In recent years, the subspecies of Self-Hating Vets known as Ivy League Self-Hating Vets has been the most active cohort of this group.

SELF-HATING VET SUBSPECIES: THE IVY LEAGUE SELF-HATING VET

The Ivy League Self-Hating Vet is closely related to but quite different in appearance from the garden-variety Self-Hating Vet. This subspecies once proclaimed solidarity with the antiwar, anti-American political agenda and indulged in the drug-hazed hippie lifestyle. But as soon as the going got tough (and the money got short), the Ivy League Self-Hating Vet fell back into the indulgent bosom of the wealthy family that paid for his Ivy League experience in the first place. Though the Ivy League Self-Hating Vet served in Nam, he never really felt comfortable with his fellow "nam polloi" and eventually settled into a life of wealth, ease, and vaguely liberal politics. The Ivy League Self-Hating Vet believes strongly in liberal causes, as long as they don't interfere with his cash flow or his summers spent jet skiing on the East Coast.

The Ivy League Self-Hating Vet doesn't smoke as much pot as other Self-Hating Vets (smoking harms the environment), but he is potentially much more dangerous since he can delude people in political discussions with his coiffed, well-groomed appearance, patrician manner, and well-modulated voice. The Ivy League Self-Hating Vet can be found on college campuses, teaching alternative histories of the United States in American Studies departments. Some inhabit the halls of the U.S. Congress, where they use their smooth social graces and try to fool the media into believing that they graduated from the University of Hard Knocks.

BEST OF BREED

- Roland Cordero was so impressed by Vietnam Veterans Against the War that he formed his own organization, Vietnam Veterans Against the War Anti-Imperialist. Cordero went as far as publishing his own magazine, the *Veteran*, and promoting his own politically skewed agenda. Unfortunately, his efforts were not appreciated by the real Vietnam Veterans Against the War, who filed suit against Vietnam Veterans Against the War Anti-Imperialist. On April 21, 1980, Judge Warren D. Wolfson signed a consent decree ordering Cordero to "refrain from deliberate efforts to represent any event, activity or endorsement as the event, activity or endorsement of Vietnam Veterans Against the War." Even today Self-Hating Vets warn unsuspecting liberals that Vietnam Veterans Against the War Anti-Imperialist is "the creation of an obscure, ultraleft sect, designed to confuse people in order to associate themselves with VVAW's many years of activism and struggle."

- Al Gore, the former vice president, is an exemplary Ivy League Self-Hating Vet specimen. The scion of a wealthy southern media family, Gore eschewed a life of wealth and privilege to work as a reporter in Vietnam, only to return to a life of wealth and privilege and liberal politics. After serving as President Bill Clinton's wing man for eight years, Gore struck out on his own quest for the presidency, eventually losing the race to fellow Ivy League graduate George W. Bush. Today, Gore has reinvented himself once again, as the Ivy League Self-Hating Vet who is the head of a wealthy southern media empire that makes millions of dollars producing documentaries about global warming and other liberal entertainments.

POSTER BOY

Scott Camil, a truly radical Self-Hating Vet leader, attended a meeting of Vietnam Veterans Against the War in November 1971 and made a mild-mannered suggestion—assassinate U.S. senators John Tower, Strom Thurmond, and John Stennis. Others at the meeting thought Camil was joking about what he called "The Phoenix Project," but he wasn't. "I was serious," Camil later confessed. "I felt that I spent two years killing women and children in their own f*&%ing homes. These are the guys that f*&%ing made the policy, and these were the guys that were responsible for it, and these were the guys that were voting to continue the f*&%ing war when the public was against it." For some reason, other members of the Vietnam Veterans Against the War, including John Kerry, voted down the plan.

HANDLING TIPS

- *Level One (couch commando)*—Get into a history discussion with a Self-Hating Vet, and then mention in passing the "Legalize Marijuana Smoke-In" going on on the other side of the city. By the time he completes the fool's errand, the protest will be over.
- *Level Two (fairly concerned citizen)*—Get an American South Vietnamese war refugee to shake the Self-Hating Vet's hand and thank him for his military service.
- *Level Three (ProtestWarrior)*—Just let him be. The confused and tired Self-Hating Vet has been through enough.

ACID FREAKS

FEELING IT

CONTENTS
UNKNOWN

SURPRISINGLY GOOD
HAND-EYE COORDINATION

CHAPTER 12

||||||||||||||||||||||||||||||||||||||||||||||||||||||

ACID FREAKS

Acid Freak: The jester of the protest world, the Acid Freak inhabits a parallel universe inspired by drugs, utopian fantasies, or exotic religious visions—and enjoys entertaining people with his manifest insanity.

IDENTIFYING CHARACTERISTICS

Acid Freaks are easily identified by their colorful garb, burned-out appearance, and freakish behavior. Casualties of the sixties, they may be wearing any type of clothing—from rainbow-colored T-shirts to ponchos to flowing skirts to East Indian–style shirts to Apache loincloths. When an Acid Freak summons his faculties to speak what's on his mind, it's usually paranoid gibbering nonsense. The Acid Freak is subconsciously aware that he's not getting through to anyone, so he mostly keeps the thoughts swirling through his head to himself.

Acid Freaks, as their name suggests, appear to be on a lifelong trip, never quite emerging from an altered state of reality where colors, objects, and ideas merge in ways they just aren't supposed to. When this altered state is applied to political philosophy, the Acid Freak leans toward the left, naturally. However, what separates Acid Freaks from the rest of the protest species is their serene indifference. Sure they want Bush out of the White House, sure they want free health care for all, and if they ever gave it a thought, they would be for higher taxes for the rich. But Acid Freaks know none of this will ever change them or their freaky lifestyle, one way or the other.

THE ORIGIN OF THE SPECIES

Free spirits, Dionysians, hard partiers, call them what you will, Acid Freaks have been partying on the fringes of political systems for millennia. Earlier generations of Acid Freaks left few records as they were too trashed to care about what they were doing the next day, much less to care about posterity. Acid Freaks began to emerge in the artistic circles of the eighteenth century, as rich patrons indulged their entertaining lifestyles. The Beat generation, poets, writers, drunks, and drug addicts were the forerunners of today's Acid Freaks. Allen Ginsberg built the bridges between the gay literary scene of City Lights Bookstore in San Francisco and the liberal protesters of the 1960s, which gave rise to the Yippies, the clown princes of liberal protesters in the sixties. Ginsberg also helped lead American Acid Freaks to India, where they thought they met kindred spirits in a select few saddhus or holy men—whacked-out, long-haired religious and social radicals, many of whom lived naked—Indian versions of the Acid Freak.

The commune push in the late 1960s attracted Acid Freaks to colonies around the country, where tripping on acid was part of the everyday routine. These communes continued to spawn generations of protest-loving exhibitionists, and acid soon gave way to pot (even though the brain damage was already done). The Acid Freaks soon embraced reggae music and the dreadlocked philosophy of Rastafarianism drifting up from Jamaica in the late seventies.

Dancing, drumming, singing, chanting, and most of all smoking lots and lots of pot, Acid Freaks are as much a part of liberal protests as corn dogs are a part of carnivals. When things get really desperate, liberals always grab for television time by sending in the Acid Freaks—or at least introducing them to TV reporters desperate for cute or funny visuals.

BEHAVIOR

Acid Freaks will do anything that's considered way outside the mainstream—chanting, dancing, taking their clothes off, chanting mystic syllables, or sitting very, very still for long periods of time in muddy waters. Why do they act this way? Acid Freaks often believe that they are the centers of the universe and that they can control the destiny of fellow men and nations by their own quasispiritual activities. During protest marches, they tend to stay at the fringes, chanting or banging on drums. Some Acid Freaks hold protests all by themselves—on street corners, or near fountains, or in their friends' living rooms. Some Acid Freaks cross-dress—not because they're sexually confused, just because they're confused period. Female Acid Freaks wear flowing skirts and have ridiculously long hair. Female Acid Freaks are usually more entrepreneurial than the males. They can often be spotted selling T-shirts, poorly handcrafted jewelry, honey, radishes, or anything. When not selling wares, many female Acid Freaks spend their time spinning around to music no one can hear with their arms making intricate movements as they cut through the air.

Acid Freaks often garden or try to farm, although usually they are best at growing killer hydroponic sinsemilla or cute little colonies of psilocybin mushrooms. Acid Freaks make a lot of noise, though they sometimes refer to it as music. They like to play drums, often in circles and usually out of rhythm. More annoying than the drums, some Acid Freaks play the didgeridoo, an instrument from Australia that sounds like a one-note bagpipe with asthma. Acid Freaks are often smiling, laughing, or at least seem to be enjoying themselves. The fact that strange actions don't change the course of the world does not seem to frustrate Acid Freaks at all. In fact, they take it as a cosmic joke.

HABITAT

Physically, Acid Freaks appear at random times and in random locations at protest marches, depending on which spiritual entity is giving them directions. Mentally, they seem to inhabit the outer limits of the liberal protester universe. You can see them, but they can't see you. Acid Freaks are at their best in large group meetings of other Acid Freaks. Taking Woodstock as the model, Acid Freaks continue to gather at rock festivals around the country. Wherever the police decide it is too much trouble to enforce public drug consumption laws stringently, there you will find Acid Freaks.

The Rainbow Family Gathering (known as the "Family") gained infamy as the unofficial American Acid Freak convention, the Super Bowl of freakdom, where Acid Freaks from around the country gathered to celebrate their individuality with other Acid Freaks who looked like them, acted like them, and were also celebrating their individuality. Of course, there are no official leaders or structure or spokespersons, and no membership is required. Instead, the community is brought together by their shared "traditions" of love for the Earth, gatherings to pray for peace, and of course, to do lots of drugs. It is maintained by councils consisting of any "nonmember" who wishes to be part of the council. Every year they gather in some U.S. forest and aggravate forest service workers who have to clean up their mess. A few isolated Acid Freaks live in rusted Volkswagen vans or Impala station wagons filled with incredibly important back issues of the *New York Times* and *Popular Mechanics*. As a rule, Acid Freaks don't make good neighbors.

SIGNS AND SLOGANS

The Ethiopian flag, symbolizing the Rasta religion, or anything with the colors of the Ethiopian flag, green, gold, and red.

Dancing bears, a symbol for Owsley Stanley III, also known as the Bear, one of the early LSD manufacturers who was also the soundman for the Grateful Dead.

Support Whirled Peas

Nobody for President

SOUNDTRACK SELECTION

Acid Freaks don't really like songs with a beginning, middle, or end, and will only listen to jams. Jam bands that have been particularly popular with Acid Freaks over the years include the Grateful Dead, Phish, and String Cheese Incident. Acid Freaks also enjoy the albums of Bob Marley and the Wailers.

THE PARTY LINE

"There were philosophers and philanthropists, bankrupt merchants and broken-down grocery keepers; officers who had retired from the Texan army on half pay; and some who had retired from situations in New York ten-pin alleys. There were all kinds of ideas, notions, theories and whims; all kinds of religion; and some persons without any. There was no unanimity of purpose, nor congeniality of disposition." (Description of commune founded in 1840s by Albert Brisbane with the support of liberal media magnate Horace Greeley)

BETWEEN THE LINES

It was a total disaster.

IN THEIR OWN WORDS

1. The blending of pot and politics into a political grass leaves movement—a cross-fertilization of the hippie and New Left philosophies.
2. A connecting link that would tie together as much of the underground as was willing into some gigantic national get-together.
3. The development of a model for an alternative society.
4. The need to make some statement, especially in action-theater terms, about the Democratic Party, electoral politics, and the state of the nation.

—The objectives of the Yippies as recorded in
Revolution for the Hell of It (1968)

"We are all the same person trying to shake hands with our self."

—Wavy Gravy

TIMELINE

1841—John Humphrey Noyes, a free-loving Dartmouth graduate and a lawyer from Vermont, establishes a commune in Oneida, New York. While Noyes is forced to leave, the commune thrives by making silverware.

1841—Brook Farm founded by Unitarian ministers near Boston. Manual labor was wedded with intellectual endeavors and "the weeds were scratched out of the ground to the music of Tennyson and Browning." The commune did not last long.

1956—Allen Ginsberg's epic poem *Howl* banned for obscenity in San Francisco. The ban was lifted when a judge ruled that the poem had redeeming social importance.

1966—Timothy Leary founds the League for Spiritual Discovery to promote LSD as a psychedelic route to a mystical transcendent experience—and partial dementia.

1967—Allen Ginsberg leads a protest in Washington during which Ginsberg tries to levitate the Pentagon by chanting the syllable "Om" with a small group. It didn't work.

1967—The Yippies form from a group of people who are sitting around Abbie Hoffman's New York City apartment smoking pot. The name Yippies supposedly came from a stoned interpretation of the two-fingered peace salute and an explanation conjured up for the press that it meant Youth International Party. The Yippies hold a Festival of Life at the 1968 Democratic convention with the "intention to bring thousands of young people to Chicago . . . to groove on rock bands and smoke grass and then put them up against bayonets." The Festival of Life turns into a riot of hate with multiple injuries, arrests, and mayhem.

1969—First Woodstock Music and Art Festival held on a farm in Bethel, New York. Five hundred thousand people attend the festival, although many millions claim to have been there.

1975—Haile Selassie I, emperor of Ethiopia, known before his coronation as Ras Tafari Makonnen, revered as the living God incarnate, called Jah, by followers of the Rasta faith, dies. His death is not accepted by many loyal followers, who believe that the death was a hoax, and Haile Selassie will return to liberate his people.

1977—Yippie Aron Kay hits anti-gay-rights activist Anita Bryant in the face with a pie. Kay later pies William F. Buckley, G. Gordon Liddy, and Randall Terry, and inspires the Biotic Baking Brigade to pie Ann Coulter, David Horowitz, and others.

1999—"Woodstock 1999" rock festival held in upstate New York to recapture the "peace and love" vibe of the original Woodstock. Things started to get a little out of hand when participants destroyed many water fountains, and the remaining fountains were guarded by "mud people," who would throw mud at anyone wishing access to the available water. What with poor sanitation, security, and the ninety-degree heat, the situation got dicey. Recognizing the potential danger, many food and water vendors requested permission to sell their goods at cost, but the Woodstock organizers refused. After the band Red Hot Chili Peppers passed out candles to the crowd, peace turned to pyromania, as the crowd ignited bonfires, destroyed a dozen trailers, looted vendor booths, destroyed ATMs, and raped at least four women. Before the riot, the band Rage Against the Machine burned an American flag onstage.

BEST OF BREED

- Timothy Leary (1920–96)—The "high priest of LSD" was a Harvard psychologist who began experimenting with "magic mushrooms" in 1960, ingesting psilocybin at weekend getaways with his students. When faculty and parents became concerned, Leary was fired in 1963, traveled to India in 1965, then lived in a teepee on an estate outside New York City and gave lectures in which he predicted that the United States "will be an LSD country within fifteen years." Convicted of drug possession, Leary escaped to Africa, Europe, and Afghanistan where the authorities finally turned him over to the United States. Leary served time in prison before declaring that "the PC is the LSD of the nineties." But the visuals aren't quite as good, man.

- Wavy Gravy (born Hugh Romney, 1936)—The "official clown" of the band the Grateful Dead was in charge of security at the first Woodstock with his Hog Farm Collective. When asked what tools he would use to enforce the rules, Gravy responded, "Cream pies and seltzer bottles." The founder of the Hog Farm, which he describes as a "mobile, hallucination-extended family," Wavy Gravy once observed, "The nineties are the sixties standing on their head."

- Abbie Hoffman (1936–89)—A former civil rights activist, Hoffman helped found the Youth International Party (Yippies), and in 1967 threw fistfuls of mostly fake money from the gallery of the New York Stock Exchange. At the 1968 Democratic Convention in Chicago, Hoffman and the other Yippies threatened to drop LSD into the city's water supply, hijack the Chicago office of Nabisco and distribute free cookies, and run naked through the streets. At Woodstock, Hoffman grabbed the microphone but was attacked by the Who's guitarist Pete Townshend. Hoffman ran out of jokes in 1973, when he was arrested on drug charges, went underground, and resurfaced as a journalist.

- Ken Kesey (1935–2001)—Bestselling author and LSD enthusiast, Kesey studied journalism at the University of Oregon. In 1959, he volunteered to be part of a study on psychoactive drugs, which inspired him in part to write his best-known novel, *One Flew Over the Cuckoo's Nest* (1962). Arrested for marijuana possession in 1966, Kesey hightailed it to Mexico, then later hightailed it across the country in a bus with the Merry Pranksters, an adventure described in Tom Wolfe's book *The Electric Kool-Aid Acid Test*.

- Allen Ginsberg (1926–97)—The bard of the Acid Freaks was an outspoken homosexual who fell in with Jack Kerouac, William S. Burroughs, and other Beat writers while a student at Columbia in the

1940s. Best known for his 1956 poem *Howl*, an epic dealing with how consumer society promotes evil values, Ginsberg was deported from Cuba in 1965 for saying that Marxist revolutionary leader "Che" Guevara was "cute." Ginsberg later founded the Jack Kerouac School of Disembodied Poetics at Naropa University in Boulder, Colorado.

HANDLING TIPS

- *Level One/Two/Three*—Go up to an Acid Freak and ask him if he has looked at his hand lately. Four hours later, you will find him glued to the same spot, looking at his hand.

DYLAN WANNABES

WAILING

FOR SALE

CHAPTER 13

||||||||||||||||||||||||||||||||||||||||||||||||||||||||||||||||||||||||||||||||||||||||

DYLAN WANNABES

Dylan Wannabe: A musician with no imagination, no talent, and no stage presence whose goal in life is to change the world—and resemble Bob Dylan circa 1963 as closely as possible.

IDENTIFYING CHARACTERISTICS

Dylan Wannabes make themselves very easy to spot, since they do everything they can to get noticed. Up on the stage with their guitar in front of the protest rally crowd is where they want to be, though very few fulfill this lifelong dream. Most are relegated to playing to the protest passersby and hawking their latest CD, which they just burned on their friend's laptop. Most Dylan Wannabes show a startling lack of originality in their fashion choice and wear a blue-collar denim button-down long-sleeve work shirt with double pockets. Rayban sunglasses or Lennon-style spectacles are common. Of course, all of them have an acoustic guitar strapped around their neck and some of the more serious specimens splurge for the accompanying harmonica support. To compete with the unavoidable noise that typifies a protest, Dylan Wannabes will sometimes use a heavy-duty pawn-shop-bought amplifier, adding to the cacophony.

THE ORIGIN OF THE SPECIES

The sounds of drums, bugles, fifes, and other martial instruments have inspired troops defending their national honor for centuries, but the whine of nasal vocals and spit-soaked harmonicas has been the musical score for liberal protests for only the last four decades. Where did this strangely dissonant muse of the left come from? Most Dylan Wannabes will say that they sing folk music, the real music of the people. But what kind of folk are we talking about? The Dylan Wannabe is the direct musical descendant of a handful of white music makers who managed to be branded as the voice of the people. Woody Guthrie was the godfather of the American lefty whine. Guthrie in turn begat Pete Seeger and Bob Dylan, who in turn begat (to paraphrase a Dylan line) a thousand telephones that would not ring and a thousand singers who could not sing.

Joe Hill (1879–1915), another prominent predecessor to the species, wrote songs for the *Little Red Song Book*—an annual published by the Industrial Workers of the World, the ultimate in radical unions. Hill supplemented his income as a songwriter with petty burglaries and was picked up for the murder of a grocery store owner and his son. The evidence was circumstantial, but enough to get Hill the death penalty and a permanent place as a martyr for liberal causes. But at least Hill had a sense of humor. When asked by the court whether he wished to be executed by firing squad or hanging, Joe Hill quipped, "I'll take the shooting. I've been shot a couple of times before, and I think I can take it."

In recent years, the female Dylan Wannabe has come into prominence, with roots tied to Dylan himself, through Dylan's onetime paramour Joan Baez. Baez, Joni Mitchell, and Judy Collins led the throng of female Dylan Wannabes, some of whom have recently focused on lesbian activism, a cause the great Dylan himself has never taken up. For some reason, leftist political organizers seem to believe that no protest is complete without the performance of a Dylan Wannabe.

BEHAVIOR

All you have to do to find a Dylan Wannabe at a liberal protest is follow your ears to the sounds that bear some resemblance to melodies with lyrics that hold some resemblance to English. Though most Dylan Wannabes struggle with chord progression, melody, and rhythm, they all exhibit an attitude of defiant assurance. Dylan Wannabes firmly believe that what they are singing may not sound all that good, but their message is VERY, VERY IMPORTANT, and they lack any appreciation of Dylan's sense of humor. They sing about TRUTH and JUSTICE and are sure that anyone listening will be moved by the sincere quiver in their voice. When they aren't singing in public, they are tuning their guitars. Many Dylan Wannabes actually spend more of their performance time tuning their guitar, changing guitar strings, and adjusting their annoying harmonica holders than they do actually playing music. Some Dylan Wannabes don't even bother with instruments as complicated as guitars or harmonicas. This is the extremely pathetic subspecies called Wannabe Dylan Wannabes—people who play tambourines or hand drums, or just clap along, usually out of rhythm with their paramour Dylan Wannabes (think Linda McCartney).

When they are not performing in public, Dylan Wannabes are writing songs. They spend hours and hours writing songs while drinking, while doing drugs, while walking along the pavement and avoiding cracks, while cooking large pots of brown rice, while waiting in line to collect unemployment—no matter what he or she is doing, the Dylan Wannabe is always working hard writing songs. The amazing thing about the Dylan Wannabe songwriting process is that no matter how long it takes, all the songs sound exactly the same. Though Bob Dylan has usually hidden his politics in a fog of poetically intriguing lyrical nonsense, the Dylan Wannabe, being vastly less creative, can only write long and dull tunes and lyrics that sound more like the talking points found on International ANSWER's website. The longer and duller the song, the more it proves that the Dylan Wannabe isn't a commercial sellout (many Dylan Wannabes believe that Dylan himself is a commercial sell-out).

HABITAT

Dylan Wannabes spend as much time as possible near microphones. They do not care that most of these microphones are attached to short-circuited amplifiers, crimped audio cables, and blown-out speakers. Dylan Wannabes don't much care if the microphone is not attached to anything at all. You can also see them behind the microphones found in bars and coffee shops, especially on open mic nights. Open mic nights provide Dylan Wannabes the opportunity to try out their new material. Of course, it sounds just like their old material, but they seem to feel the urge to try it out anyway. And the audience response to these performances is remarkably predictable—no response whatsoever, other than the sound of one pair of hands clapping, a pair of hands that belongs to a Dylan Wannabe groupie.

Microphones are also to be found at "folk festivals." These vaguely regulated handicraft and drug markets are where folk musicians perform for one another and hold all-night hootenannies around campfires singing one another's songs, which is easy because all the songs sound the same. Dylan Wannabes will often wander away from the microphone and continue to strum their guitars and sing their songs while walking with protest marchers, or just wandering through city streets or along park trails. Dylan Wannabes encountered in these open-range habitats will often smile and nod at passersby, hoping for a nod of approval in response. By all means *do not nod approval*. This will just encourage them to believe that they are on the brink of signing with a record label and they should stick to it for a few more years.

SIGNS OR SLOGANS

To Fan the Flames of Discontent (slogan of Joe Hill's *Little Red Song Book*, 1915)

This Machine Kills Fascists

SOUNDTRACK SELECTION

"Casey Jones—The Union Scab"—A good ol' head-busting union song from Joe Hill.

"This Land Is My Land"—Woody Guthrie's ode to socialism.

"A Hard Rain's a-Gonna Fall"—Dylan's prediction of a nuclear apocalypse.

"Joe Hill"—Joan Baez's anthem in praise of convicted murderer Joe Hill.

"Puff, the Magic Dragon"—Peter, Paul, and Mary's kids' song all about drugs.

THE PARTY LINE/IN THEIR OWN WORDS

"If a person can put a few cold, commonsense facts into a song and dress them . . . up in a cloak of humor to take the dryness out of them, he will succeed in reaching a great number of workers who are too unintelligent or too indifferent to read a pamphlet or an editorial on economic science."

—Joe Hill

"Folk singing is a bunch of fat people."

—Bob Dylan

REQUIRED READING (AND VIEWING)

Bound for Glory (1943), Woody Guthrie's autobiography.

Tarantula (1971), by Bob Dylan. If you can understand this book, please share your drugs with others. If you can't make any sense of it, try watching some of Dylan's movies: *Pat Garrett and Billy the Kid* (1973*)*, *Renaldo and Clara* (1978), *Hearts of Fire* (1987), and *Masked and Anonymous* (2003). If you appreciate the plot, the characters, or the writing in any of these absolutely opaque cinematic doodlings, you're in trouble.

TIMELINE

November 19, 1915—Joe Hill, songwriter and organizer for the Industrial Workers of the World, is executed by firing squad in Salt Lake City, Utah, not for his music, but for murder.

1939—Woody Guthrie moves to that down-home town in the heartland, New York City, where he at last finds an audience among leftists and folk music fans. A year later Guthrie writes his most famous song, "This Land Is Your Land," in which he asks his leftist groupies the musical question, "Is this land made for you and me?"

August 18, 1955—Pete Seeger testifies before the House Un-American Activities Committee, where he refuses to talk about his friends and political associates, perhaps because he was an outspoken member of the Communist Party until 1950. Why did he leave the party? According to Seeger, "I realized I could sing the same songs I sang whether I belonged to the Communist Party or not."

1962—Robert Allen Zimmerman legally changes his name to Bob Dylan and later observes, "I've done more for Dylan Thomas than he's ever done for me." He plays at coffeehouses in Cambridge, Massachusetts, the image forever preserved by Dylan Wannabes.

1965—Dylan plays electric guitar with a rock band during his performance at the Newport Jazz Festival. The performance and the subsequent forty years of Dylan's rock-and-roll career are ignored by all Dylan Wannabes who contend that Dylan does not wannabe Dylan.

1969—A free concert at Altamont Speedway just outside San Francisco puts an end to the Dylan Wannabe aspirations of the Rolling Stones. Instead of peace and love, Altamont results in four dead, dozens seriously injured, and two thousand drug overdoses. "You have been so groovy," Mick Jagger said at the end of the concert. "Good night."

April 2006—Dylan Wannabe Bruce Springsteen releases his folkiest CD, *We Shall Overcome: The Seeger Sessions*. Springsteen tours to support the CD with a twenty-five-piece "folk music" orchestra, a multi-million-dollar undertaking that proves Springsteen is still a member of the downtrodden proletariat.

BEST OF BREED

- Pete Seeger (b. 1919)—The son of a composer who grew up in New York City, Seeger became one of the "folk" when he heard a five-string banjo at a music festival in 1936. Having plunked his way into the Communist Party in 1942, Seeger was tried for his "subversive activities" in 1961, but his case was dismissed on a technicality. He spent most of his later years floating along the Hudson River on the sailing ship *Clearwater*, playing his banjo as often as possible.
- Joan Baez (b. 1941)—Born in New York State, Baez started singing in Harvard coffeehouses in the 1950s and performed at the Newport Folk Festival when she was just eighteen. She recorded albums that sold well, briefly dated Dylan himself, then turned her attention to protesting the Vietnam War, and in 1968 married draft resister David Harris. After her hubby spent three years in jail, they split up, and Joan later spent two stints in prison for her antiwar activities. Unlike most Dylan Wannabes, Baez can actually sing. At Woodstock she crooned, "I dreamed I saw Joe Hill last night/Alive as you and me."
- David Crosby (b. 1941)—One of the most successful Dylan Wannabes had one of his early hits in 1965, singing the Dylan song "Mr. Tambourine Man" with the Byrds. Crosby went on to sing liberal harmonies with Crosby, Stills, Nash, and Young before his appetite for drugs led to numerous arrests and jail time. Once upon a time, Crosby set himself on fire while freebasing. Today, Crosby counsels other Dylan Wannabes about drug abuse and proper parenting.

PERFORMANCE ARTISTS

CHAPTER 14

||||||||||||||||||||||||||||||||||||||||||||||||||||||||||||||||||||||||||||||||||||||||

PERFORMANCE ARTISTS

Performance Artist: A political street performer with a high degree of self-regard engaged in a grotesque "performance" to express a grotesque ideology.

IDENTIFYING CHARACTERISTICS

It is easy to pick out a Performance Artist at a protest. Just look around at the crowd. Is there a big, awkward, ready-to-collapse puppet that vaguely looks human? Are there individuals who look like they haven't changed clothes since Halloween? Are there some crude political ideas expressed with even cruder papier-mâché creations? Are there individuals in tights? Or in skull face paint? Or wearing tinfoil? These are all Performance Artists. Performance Artists can sometimes be confused with Acid Freaks, except that Acid Freaks are usually more entertaining and more talented than Performance Artists. While some Performance Artists write humorous "skits" that they act out during protests, or do interpretive dances sympathizing with the world's oppressed, most Performance Artists march in costume, letting the obvious symbolism (or whatever you want to call it) speak eloquently for whatever it is that they believe. And what is it they believe? That big puppets have political influence? That skeletons will scare conservatives into becoming liberals? That perverse sexual humor will convince people that liberal protesters don't believe in perverse sexual activity? No one is quite sure of the answers to these questions, but that doesn't mean they can't be used as a tremendous source of entertainment.

THE ORIGIN OF THE SPECIES

Street performers have a noble heritage going back to the traveling minstrels of the Middle Ages, jugglers, acrobats, and contortionists. But Performance Artists in earlier ages actually had to be able to do something exceptional—or they would starve to death. Today's street Performance Artists don't do anything but walk around in grotesque, poorly made costumes. People who can't draw, paint, write, sing, or dance did not dare call themselves artists until the twentieth century. But after the urinal as art by the French chess-playing surrealist Marcel Duchamp, after the theater of cruelty, the theater of the absurd, the happenings of the 1960s, and the conceptual art movement of the 1970s, the human race has agreed to call anything art as long as a few folks in New York City agree. Political theater used the dramatic arts to help stir up the masses before the era of broadcasting. Now the best performers are in the movies and on TV, leaving just the most pretentious in galleries, and the seriously deranged ones on the streets.

But in the modern world of politically correct liberal protests, anyone who calls himself an artist has to be considered an artist, even if he doesn't make anything. All you need is a burning hatred for your political opposition, money for costume materials, paint and papier-mâché, some very rudimentary knowledge of puppeteering, and lots and lots of time.

BEHAVIOR

Performance Artists are always angling for their Warholian fifteen minutes of fame, and very often they get it. During protests, they will do anything to get camera time, including blocking the protest from moving along the street so the cameras can get a clear shot. Performance Artists are extremely self-important. They are their own best audience, often seen laughing at themselves and their fellow artists, or so entranced by their own skills that they cannot see that no one else is watching.

Performance Artists love to revel in the subject of human suffering. However, they tend to be highly selective of which suffering humans deserve their support. One of the scenes performance artists love to stage is the bomb site, with protesters covering the ground as Afghani and Iraqi civilians accidentally killed by American or Coalition forces. Victims of the Taliban's and Saddam's regimes' intentional slaughter of civilians are given no such consideration, since these civilian casualties cannot be integrated with their blame-America paradigm. Another favorite street theater protest shtick is the Israeli "Apartheid" Wall demonstration. In this skit, performers (typically College Students) feign being imprisoned behind a symbolic wall or try to get through a "checkpoint," only to be rebuffed by a heartless IDF "soldier." Of course, these students aren't carrying any explosive belts designed to spray Israeli civilians with rat-poison-laced shrapnel, nor are they trying to smuggle surface-to-air rocket launchers.

Many times, Performance Artists behave independently of the protesters around them, preferring abstract protests of cosmic injustice to political debate or concrete discussions.

When they are not performing, performance artists spend a great deal of time writing about their own work. Long, involved, politically charged explanations accompany most Performance Artist performances, unless they are accompanied by incredibly meaningful silence. Almost anything can be charged with great significance if it is included in a performance art piece.

Obviously, the most noteworthy behavior of Performance Artists is the behavior they exhibit during their performances. And at no time in modern American political history did Performance Artists exhibit more ridiculous behavior than at the 2004 Republican National Convention in New York City. Performance behavior associated with the event included:

The Vomitorium—A theatrical performance that re-created a Roman vomitorium with a sixty-two-person volunteer cast and crew in protest of "American imperialist policies."

Howl—A performance piece with an all-female cast celebrating the power of women and "exploring the possibility that discrimination against women, the slaughter of animals, and consumerism is the fertilizer for war."

A Hot Day in Texas—Billed as "sight-specific performance reflecting on the blindly excessive oil consumption in the U.S."

Harmonic Insurgence—A choral performance art group that entertained Republican conventioneers at the entrances to four hotels with a revised version of "The Star-Spangled Banner" that replaced the words of our national anthem with the endlessly repeated phrase "Stop the War."

"I'm Going to Kill the President: A Federal Offense"—A delightful little play described in the press as a "cheerfully sophomoric satire" filled with ribald Bush jokes. The performance told the story of a terrorist name Skip who blows up his girlfriend, then accompanies Fifi (an alienated NYU coed) to a Kmart bathroom and then Guantánamo Bay. Meanwhile, a green monster symbolizing the mass media ate radical liberals and spewed them out as "consumers." The press described the performance as "beating a dead elephant."

HABITAT

Performance Artists inhabit the nether world of the arts—their own fantasy life. Since they have few skills, the least being artistic, they tend to have very low-skill jobs—or are unemployed. Unemployed Performance Artist is a heck of a résumé lead. Manhattan (especially its East Village neighborhood) is infested with Performance Artists. There are so many of them in Manhattan that they feed each other's egos and actually believe that what they are doing has some relevance. Like mosquitoes looking at bags of water, Performance Artists look much bigger in the reflection of the handful of other Performance Artists who actually take their work seriously.

THE PARTY LINE

"Our work utilizes volunteer-based public performance as a means for articulating shared ideas within our community. What began with projects that engaged the passerby in interplay with absurd, random events, developed towards the discovery of collective socio-political ideas. . . . We believe that presenting an idea through the collective art form, rather than traditional means of protest, allows for the delivery of authentic artistic and political messages to wider audiences." (Marina Potok and Wendy Tremayne, artist statement)

BETWEEN THE LINES

Since we can't really articulate our thoughts into something coherent, we prefer to express whatever's in our head via performance, leaving us open to interpretation in the small chance that what we are doing can be mistaken as "sociopolitically" relevant.

IN THEIR OWN WORDS

The preceding monologue was presented by one of the many Performance Artist mimes. Their work (and its effectiveness) speaks for itself.

BEST OF BREED

- *Women in Black*—An international antiwar activist group that encourages women to wear "sculptural costumes" and stand in silent vigil "to protest war, rape as a tool of war, ethnic cleansing, and human rights abuses all over the world." They don't speak much, and are "silent because mere words cannot express the tragedy that wars and hatred bring."
- *"Complacency: A Renegade Action"*—A piece in which Ms. Kat Skraba was delivered to Hollywood Boulevard in Los Angeles on a military

stretcher covered with a type of Saran Wrap and bound and gagged with a U.S. flag.

- *Reverend Billy & the Church of Stop Bombing*—The Church of Stop Bombing opposes bombing and shopping and believes that one causes the other. Reverend Billy "preaches" his performance art messages on street corners, at conventions, and wherever else he feels he can get an audience.
- *Bread and Puppet Theater*—Affiliated with liberal protests for decades, this group's "work" includes "Public Participation Uprising: The Insurrection Mass with Funeral March for a Rotten Idea: A Special Mass for the Aftermath of the Events of September 11," which featured several papier-mâché gods "guaranteed to have been made of garbage" and puppets that "resemble twisted fused masses of pinkish or bloodied babies."

POSTER GIRLS AND BOYS

Breasts Not Bombs—This northern California–based performance group hopes to ensnare unwitting men with a seemingly irresistible proposition. When men first hear of the group, it's a very easy choice to make: Do you want bombs or do you want to see bare-chested ladies walking in your city streets? However, they quickly learn that there's no such thing as a free lunch when they finally get a glimpse of the topless aging heifers that make up this nightmare-inducing procession. The women of Breasts Not Bombs believe that there's no sexual difference between men's and women's breasts, and stage nonviolent performance protests to underscore the connection between breast exposure equality and other weighty social issues including, as they put it, the "immoral injustices of war, its torturous prisons and obscene profits." If you haven't yet witnessed this group in action, consider yourself very lucky. And please, resist all temptation to search for their photos online. The authors of this book had to for the sake of research, but you can still walk away with your innocence intact.

Billionaires for Bush—Composed mainly of trust-fund kids overwhelmed with guilt, Billionaires for Bush caricature anyone who complains about having to hand over half his income to the government every year as a bloodthirsty parasite living off the sweat of the working-class poor. Dressed excessively aristocratically (think garden party at Jay Gatsby's) and seemingly in favor of George Bush, their entire existence serves to promote the cliché that Republicans only represent the interests of the ultrarich. Like most leftists, these monotonous satirists have a third-grade understanding of economics. Either that or they choose to ignore the obvious economic realities that would reduce their tired shtick into vile class warfare propaganda at best. The fact that an across-the-board tax cut would result in the highest absolute tax savings for those shouldering most of the burden on a steeply graduated tax system eludes them. Raised on leftist bromides their entire lives, they are certain that the best way to stimulate the economy and create jobs is by taxing the wealthy into oblivion and pouring the money into an ever-expanding slew of social programs. However, any attempt to engage in debate with these smug socialite-socialists on any one of their talking points is met with such vapid retorts as "Make Social Security Neither!" "Widen the income gap!" "Thank you for paying our fair share!" or some other debate-evading device.

Missile Dick Chicks—This bizarre group of middle-aged office secretaries rivals Breasts Not Bombs in sheer grotesqueness. In order to join this avant-garde political organization, all one has to do is wear a red, white, or blue wig; a bra over your shirt; and of course the essential crowning accessory: a "strap-on missile" on your crotch. Then, at your local protest, walk through the city streets singing the Missile Dick Chicks original "Shop in the Name of War!" and you're on your way to some pretty sophisticated political satire that would make Ben Franklin proud.

HANDLING TIPS

- *Level One (couch commando)*—No need for action. Just stay on your couch and let the trained professionals deal with it.

- *Level Two (fairly concerned citizen)*—Set up an old-style larger-size video camera on a tripod, add a fake mic boom, and watch the entire horde of street artists gather in the hopes that their high jinks might be broadcasted on TV.
- *Level Three (ProtestWarrior)*—Put on a fake explosive belt, dress up like a Fatah suicide bomber, and approach an Israeli "Apartheid" Wall or checkpoint demonstration in progress. Break through the checkpoint or walk around the wall to the Israeli side and say, "Thank you for your support. You are now all dead."

ISLAMOTHUGS

GROUPIE
(COLLEGE STUDENT SPECIES)

ARAFAT-STYLE KEFFIYEH

NOT-SO-FUNNY
DANISH HUMOR

MODIFIED ISRAELI FLAG
(MEANT TO BE TAKEN SERIOUSLY)

CHAPTER 12

||||||||||||||||||||||||||||||||||||||||||||||||||||||||||||||||||||||||||

ISLAMOTHUGS

Islamothug: A Muslim who attributes all ills (from the economy to bad breath) to the existence of the United States and Israel.

IDENTIFYING CHARACTERISTICS

The most striking feature of the Islamothug is his absolute lack of a sense of humor. A smile, a laugh, a giggle, a chuckle, or even a tee-hee—all will be conspicuously absent from his unshaven face. Anger and rage are the more common forms of expression, which can be triggered by a host of topics: Zionism, American support for Israel, the thwarting of a suicide bomber, the slightest perceived insult against the religion of Islam, or any aspect of American culture. This species is almost exclusively of Arab descent and can be easily identified by a keffiyeh worn Arafat style. However, some Islamothugs prefer the more form-fitting "Islamic Freedom Fighter" look, wrapping their keffiyeh tightly around their head (see Figure 15.1).

Sandals, dusty slacks, and button-down shirts are common—but no bright-colored sportswear (Hawaiian shirts are the mark of the devil, the worst offense of the decadent West). Islamothugs do not typically carry any signage, as they feel that the keffiyeh worn proudly on the head is enough to express their unshakeable solidarity with the Palestinian Intifada and Muslim insurgents worldwide. If anything is carried, it

Figure 15.1

will almost always be a Palestinian flag. It is extremely rare to spot a solitary Islamothug in the wild, since they require the constant company of fellow Islamothugs in order to perpetuate the mass hysteria that characterizes their mental state. Instead you will find them traveling in groups of six to twenty (called a *habeeb*). This species will frequently have an entourage of College Students and Closet Nazis following closely behind, as the Islamothug is the personification of the ideal they are fighting for. The Islamothug provides these other species with the emotional endorsement they require in order to snuff out their mind's subconscious moral objections to the raging anti-Semitism animating their lives. This is one of the few rare symbiotic (and revolting) relationships occurring naturally in the protest animal kingdom.

THE ORIGIN OF THE SPECIES

The Islamothug species has a long lineage, dating back to before World War II and starting with Mohammad Amin al-Husseini, a Palestinian

Arab nationalist. In 1936, early Islamothugs led by al-Husseini targeted Jewish colonies and kibbutzim with Arab sniping, bombing, and other pleasantries. This anti-Semitic frenzy reached a fever pitch when al-Husseini personally recruited Bosnian Muslims for the German Waffen SS, who apparently relaxed their normally stringent Aryan-only policy out of practicality (see Degenerate Progenitor, page 187).

Fortunately, the Islamothug population remained fairly scanty during these formative years. However, immediately after the creation of the state of Israel in 1948, the surrounding Muslim armies of Egypt, Syria, Transjordan, Iraq, and Lebanon attacked the fledgling state and suffered a stunning defeat at the hands of the decimated Holocaust refugees. This severely humiliating blow to the brittle collective Muslim ego was the prime catalyst of the exponential population explosion in the Islamothug species as Muslims worldwide felt personally insulted that Israel had simply refused to keel over and die. This seminal year marked the beginning of a now long-standing tradition where totalitarian Muslim theocracies would invade Israel expecting a swift annihilation of the Jewish state only to find out once again that their previous defeat wasn't a fluke. This "cycle of humiliation" gave angry Muslims across the world someone to blame for the miserable and impoverished societies they had managed to produce. And Israel's steadfast American-supported presence as an example of a successful, vibrant, prosperous, and free society in the heart of the Middle East only serves to exacerbate their fervor. Where before only a few handfuls of Islamothugs would gather in the streets to praise a new dictator who had risen to power in a bloody coup (until they were imprisoned or killed by their new glorious ruler), now thousands could rally behind a cause they could really sink their teeth into: the hatred of the United States ("Big Satan") and Israel ("Little Satan").

And the population growth of Islamothugs shows no signs of slowing, as indoctrination begins at a very young age and is implemented thoroughly by the child's family, schoolteachers, and government-controlled media. Jews are depicted as depraved creatures on television and in print, newspapers publish articles claiming that matzos are made with the blood of Gentile children, Israel is removed from the map in school textbooks, and martyrdom is encouraged as a meaningful and righteous path a child should follow. As the child grows up in the miserable and impoverished societies that are the only possible consequence of a Muslim theocracy, the rulers responsible are all too happy to provide a scapegoat.

FRIGHTENING FACTOID

Islamothugs are currently the most abundant species of protester worldwide.

BEHAVIOR

Much of an Islamothug's belligerence stems from an intense insecurity over the blatantly disastrous results of the societies implemented under Islamic law. In fact, the intensity of an Islamothug's dementia is in direct proportion to his country's misery index. An Islamothug's behavior at a protest can vary greatly depending on his geographical location. Those who are interested in observing Islamothugs in the wild should do so *only in designated Western countries*. If you find yourself in a Muslim country and see a *habeeb* approaching, it is recommended that you walk away immediately (running is recommended if you are Jewish). While in Western countries, Islamothugs' rage is kept in check by the rule of law (France being the only exception—see pages 188–89) and is mostly expressed through the carrying of Palestinian flags, anti-American and anti-Israel signage, and sporadic yet spirited shrieking of "Jihad!" (Holy War), "Allahu Akbar!" (God is great), or the gold standard of chants: "Long live the Intifada!" However, while protesting in a Muslim country, Islamothugs are given generous latitude with their freedom of expression, as long as that expression remains strictly of their hatred of the twin devils from the West. For instance, while Palestinian flags are abundant, Israeli and American flags will also be carried. However, these flags are quickly incinerated in the center of a frothing Islamo mosh pit of AK-47s and primal screaming. Another marked difference between an Islamothug's behavior when in a Muslim country is the rambunctious firing of bullets randomly into the sky (typically done while howling "Allahu Akbar!"). This is one of the very few forms of momentary relief an Islamothug can get from his all-consuming obsession.

It is observed that Islamothugs are most active immediately after a calamity befalls the United States, Israel, or any other Western country. While the civilized world mourned the loss of thousands of American civilians on September 11, 2001, Palestinian Islamothugs were filmed in Lebanon, the West Bank, and East Jerusalem dancing in the streets, passing out candy to children, honking horns, and firing bullets into the air. Recognizing the potential PR damage such a sight could cause, the Palestinian Authority forcibly confined foreign journalists to a Nablus hotel, guarded by armed Palestinians, while festivities took place in the streets outside. Regarding the news reporters who were still at large, Arafat aide Ahmed Abdel Rahman told AP representatives in Jerusalem that the Palestinian Authority "cannot guarantee the life" of any cameraman whose footage was broadcast, an example of why totalitarian regimes view "freedom of the press" and other "Western" concepts as major frustrations.

During times of war, Islamothugs will conduct staged civilian funeral processions in front of news cameras to garner sympathy from

Figure 15.2: Staged funeral procession

Western television viewers (see Figure 15.2). However, every once in a while an eager and excited "pallbearer" will misstep and cause the actor to roll out of the coffin or off the stretcher and rise from the dead, making for perfect *Funniest Home Videos* material (if the Muslim world allowed entertainment television). When watching these accidental antics on video (which you can find online by Googling "Palestinian staged funeral procession"), it is recommended that you play *The Benny Hill Show* theme song in the background for maximum comic effect.

A special-case behavior of the Islamothug can be observed in the West Bank and Gaza, where the malevolence reaches such an extreme level that innocent passersby can get lynched. On September 28, 2000, Tuvia Grossman, a twenty-year-old Jewish student from Chicago, while visiting Israel, took a cab with a couple of friends to go visit the Western Wall in Jerusalem. When the driver decided to take a shortcut through one of the Muslim neighborhoods, they found themselves surrounded by a frothing mob of forty Palestinian Islamothugs. Within seconds, all of the windows of the cab were smashed in, and Tuvia was yanked out of the vehicle and pummeled by the mob. After getting punched and kicked in the face and repeatedly stabbed in the leg, he was held down while they began to smash rocks into his head. Eight minutes into the attack, after losing three pints of blood and about to lose consciousness, Tuvia managed to yell out at the top of his lungs and startle the Islamothugs just enough to allow him to break away and run. He made it to a gas station where Israeli soldiers were posted, and a snapshot was taken by a freelance photographer showing Tuvia's terrified, bloody face in front of a screaming Israeli soldier. Two days later the Associated Press distributed the photo with the caption "An Israeli Policeman and a Palestinian on the Temple Mount," leading readers to assume Tuvia was a Palestinian victim of Israeli brutality. The photo was used extensively to generate sympathy for the Palestinian Intifada.

Cartoon Riots—From February through March 2006, the Islamothug species shocked even the most educated protest behaviorists, as riots erupted across the Middle East and Europe. Islamothugs stoned U.S.

DEGENERATE PROGENITOR: MOHAMMAD AMIN AL-HUSSEINI

The Islamothug lineage begins with one man: Mohammad Amin al-Husseini, the "Grand Mufti" of Jerusalem. Al-Husseini first rose to prominence by eliminating those he considered a threat to his control of Jerusalem's Arab population, heavily utilizing anti-Jewish propaganda to polarize the two communities and inciting anti-Jewish riots by claiming the Jews were plotting to destroy the Al Aqsa mosque.

After he led the 1936 Arab revolt against the British in which he ordered armed Arab militias to massacre Jewish citizens, British forces expelled al-Husseini and he fled to Nazi Germany. There, he was pleasantly surprised to find such compatibility between Hitler's worldview and Islam: anti-Semitism, the quest for world dominance, the demand for total subordination of the individual, the belief in totalitarian government, and spittle-laden demagoguery.

Upon becoming bosom buddies with the Nazi Führer, al-Husseini helped seal the fate of European Jews, most notably preventing Adolf Eichmann's deal with the Red Cross to exchange Jewish children for German POWs. His enthusiasm and zest for the Third Reich led him to recruit Bosnian Muslims for the German Waffen SS, including the Hanjer Division, which was responsible for the murder of over 90 percent of the Yugoslavian Jewish population.

SS leader Heinrich Himmler was so pleased with al-Husseini's Muslim Nazis that he established the Dresden-based Mullah Military School for their continued recruitment and training. After the fall of Nazi Germany, al-Husseini took refuge in Cairo, Egypt, in 1946 where he continued his operations.

Refusing to retire from the Islamothug lifestyle in his old age, he became the spiritual mentor of the first PLO chairthug and saw that much of his ideology was instilled in the organization. Almost thirty years after al-Husseini's death in 1974, he is still revered as a hero by Islamothugs around the world.

and other Western embassies in Indonesia and Pakistan and *burned down* Danish and Norwegian embassies in Syria, Lebanon, and Iran. One hundred thirty-nine people were killed as a result of the riots, and almost a thousand were injured. The cause of the deadly upheaval? Cartoon caricatures of the Muslim prophet Muhammad were published by the Danish newspaper *Jyllands-Posten* (the cartoon of Muhammad with a bomb in his turban being the most controversial). Intended as criticism of radical Islam, these cartoons were taken as grave personal insults to Islamothugs everywhere and Muslim leaders passed death sentences on all cartoonists involved. Haji Yaqoob Qureishi, a minister in the Mulayam Singh Yadav government, announced a cash reward of $11 million for anyone who beheaded any of the satirists. Stand-up comedians across the Middle East took this as a cue to avoid any Muhammad material (no matter how funny), and plans to create an Arabic version of *The Simpsons* were immediately canceled.

HABITAT

Islamothugs can be found wherever there is enough critical mass to protest against the United States or Israel. In other words: in every Muslim country, all of Europe, and a few major U.S. cities. Of course, most of the world's Islamothug population is concentrated in the Middle East, where they are fed a steady diet of government instituted anti-Israel and anti-American propaganda. However, they still manage to thrive in Western societies, even though these societies represent the direct antithesis to the Islamothugs' ideology. In fact, the more "progressive" the Western country, the more brazen and hostile the Islamothug's behavior. This is the unavoidable consequence of the leftist beliefs that no one culture is better than another culture and that Israel is an aggressor and occupier, and of their denial of Islam's ultimate goal of world domination. For example, France, the progressive country par excellence, has encouraged more Islamothuggery than any other Western nation. Synagogues get Molotov cocktails thrown at their entrances,

Jewish cemeteries are regularly vandalized with spray paint and tombstones are broken, local Jewish-owned shops are bombed, and Jews are regularly assaulted in the streets by Islamothug gangs. The French government and society hesitate to criticize the Muslim leadership or those responsible for fear of a riot, encouraging other Muslims to emigrate. With a population that is 10 percent Muslim, France currently has the highest proportion of Muslims in Western Europe. In the United States, Islamothugs often live in run-down neighborhoods in Queens.

CALLS OR SLOGANS

Palestine will be free, from the river to the sea!
Black, red, brown, white! We support Hezbollah's fight!
Black, red, green, blue! We support Hamas, too!
Zionism = Nazism
End the occupation from Palestine to Iraq!

THE PARTY LINE

We are committed to resisting the illegal, immoral, and brutal Israeli occupation of Palestinian land (Gaza and the West Bank) using nonviolent, direct action. We demand recognition of the right of return with compensation for all Palestinian refugees and that Israel be charged with war crimes. As Israel violates international law by engaging in gross and systematic human rights abuses against Palestinians, we call for an immediate end to U.S. military and economic aid to Israel.

BETWEEN THE LINES/IN THEIR OWN WORDS

"Half a million martyrdom shaheed is enough for Muslims to control the whole of earth forever. In the end of the day, Islam must control earth, whether we like it or not."

—Abu Hamza al-Masri, Islamic cleric

"The greatest enemies of the Islamic nation are the Jews. . . . All spears should be directed at the Jews . . . Allah has described them as apes and pigs . . . nothing will deter them except for us voluntarily detonating ourselves in their midst. . . . Blessings for whoever has saved a bullet in order to stick it in a Jew's head."

—Sheik Ibrahim Madhi, Palestinian
Authority television, August 3, 2001

"Despite all the conspiracies, Jerusalem and Palestine from the river to the sea will remain Islamic until judgment day."

—Ikrama Sabri, Palestinian Authority
mufti of Jerusalem, May 9, 1997

"Islam isn't in America to be equal to any other faiths, but to become dominant. The Koran . . . should be the highest authority in America, and Islam the only accepted religion on Earth."

—Omar Ahmad, Council on American Islamic Relations (CAIR)

REQUIRED READING

The Koran

The Myth of Islamic Tolerance: How Islamic Law Treats Non-Muslims, Robert Spencer, ed. (2005)

HANDLING TIPS

- *Level One (couch commando)*—Take a copy of the Koran to a protest, and ask an Islamothug to translate Surah 9:5 to English: *"Slay the idolaters wherever you find them, and take them captives and besiege them and lie in wait for them in every ambush."* Then watch as backpedaling, stammering, and spinning ensue.
- *Level Two (fairly concerned citizen)*—Infiltrate a staged funeral procession and tip over the coffin. After the performer rolls out and gets up, demand that he pay you the money you loaned him, and tell him that his playing dead isn't fooling *anyone*.

- *Level Three (ProtestWarrior)*—Walk into the center of an Islamothug *habeeb*, holding the following sign:

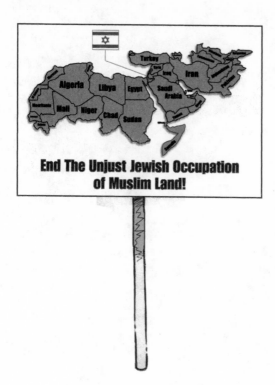

After you are met with high-fives and spirited agreement, explain the sarcastic nature of the sign.

CLOSET NAZIS

GIFT FROM HUBBY

How much longer shall America spill **GOY** blood to feed the **ZIONIST** MENACE?

HIDEOUS SIGNAGE

HIDEOUS FASHION SENSE

CHAPTER 16

‖‖‖‖‖‖‖‖‖‖‖‖‖‖‖‖‖‖‖‖‖‖‖‖‖‖‖‖‖‖‖‖‖‖‖‖‖‖

CLOSET NAZIS

Closet Nazi: An Anglo-American who hides behind incessant political criticism of Israel to mask a seething anti-Semitism.

IDENTIFYING CHARACTERISTICS

This appallingly drab species is the least fashion-conscious of all protesters. In fact, it is not uncommon for their wardrobe to be stocked exclusively from Wal-Mart. Fannypacks, embroidered sun visors, denim shorts—all are fair game to this species. Closet Nazis don't have many friends and are usually found walking in a protest alone, *always* with their sign in hand (their pride and joy). However, if they're married, their husband or wife will usually be tagging along in support. Female Closet Nazis, who are typically obese, are equal in number to their male counterparts, who tend to be slender and gaunt. If it wasn't for their bizarre and disturbing call signs, Closet Nazis would be somewhat difficult to detect. Their signs are usually much larger in size (three feet by four feet or larger) than most others you'll find at a protest, and are usually detailed and extravagantly ornate. However, these are not the elements that set them apart—it's the message on the signs they tote that has spurred political anthropologists to classify them as a separate species.

The message almost always targets Zionism and Israel with a

Figure 16.1: They mean business

bellicosity slightly reminiscent of World War II Germany (see Figure 16.1). Many times their message is framed in a manner that purports to protect American interests allegedly threatened by Israel's meddling in U.S. affairs. Signs that claim Washington is being controlled by Tel Aviv or that the U.S. leadership is puppeteered by a Jewish Neocon cabal are common.

In essence, Closet Nazis are conspiracy theorists run amok with anger. They would be much less annoying if they stuck to black helicopters, alien invasions, or Freemasons, and left the anti-Semitism to the outright fascists. You will also find this species desperately tagging along with the Islamothugs (see Chapter 15), as Islamothugs provide the Closet Nazi with verification (however weak) of the Jews' harmful effects and worldwide domination.

THE ORIGIN OF THE SPECIES

While there is very little agreement on what has caused anti-Semitism to exist since the beginning of religion, there is consensus that the book *The Protocols of the Elders of Zion* was the first widespread propaganda tool anti-Semites used to foment Jew-hatred in the modern era. The book first made its appearance in the early twentieth century and has since been repeatedly debunked as a hoax. The authors of *The Protocols* had learned an important propaganda lesson from Martin Luther's anti-Semitic screed *On the Jews and Their Lies* (published three centuries earlier, in 1543). Where Luther's book openly called for Christians to destroy all synagogues and Jewish prayer books, confiscate all property and money belonging to Jews, smash Jewish homes, and force the "poisonous envenomed worms" into labor or expel them "for all time," *The Protocols* employed a much simpler, more powerful strategy: expose to the world what the Jews were up to and let readers draw their own conclusions about what ought to be done about it. *The Protocols* purports to be an actual manual given to a new "Elders of Zion" member and explains specifically by what steps the Jewish Elders will succeed in controlling the world (by distracting the "goyim/non-Jews" with alcohol, porn, world wars, economic depression, communism, illusions of freedom, and so on). *The Protocols* pushed all the "right" buttons—racism, classism, and fear—and was a huge hit with early-nineteenth-century dictators. They would have them mass-printed and pumped out to the public whenever they needed a scapegoat for their society's ills. This tactic really caught fire in Russia before the revolution and spurred pogroms to sweep across the nation.

Adolf Hitler, the most famous purveyor of *The Protocols*, made the book required reading for German students and used it as a guide for his goal of exterminating the Jewish race. Henry Ford, founder of the Ford Motor Company, was also a fan of the book and published it in its entirety in his newspaper, the *Dearborn Independent*, throughout the 1920s (see Best of the Breed on page 201). Ford was so worked up about the subject and so convinced of the authenticity of the book that he began to write his own treatise on the matter, titled *The International Jew: The World's Foremost Problem*. When asked by the baffled press about his anti-Semitism, Ford said, "The only statement I care to make about *The Protocols* is that they fit in with what is going on." Such prominent figures felt at ease being openly anti-Semitic, as there was no strong stigma attached to that position at the time. It was only after World War II and the Holocaust that most of the *Protocols* enthusiasts decided to keep their thoughts in the closet, as Jews worldwide were a bit touchy over having half their population wiped out.

Most Closet Nazis consider July 29, 1958, the birthday of the species. That was the day on which Closet Nazi forefather George Lincoln Rockwell marched in front of the White House with the protest sign SAVE IKE FROM THE KIKES. Accompanied by a caricature of a Jew holding a gun to Eisenhower's head, his sign was intended to protest President Eisenhower's decision to send troops into the Middle East. Although this stunt would be considered a bit too racially overt, it served as encouragement for future Closet Nazis who shared Rockwell's belief that *The Protocols* were real and the world was being controlled by nefarious and clandestine Jewish masterminds. As the stigma for anti-Semitism was as strong as it had ever been, early Closet Nazis voiced their worldview carefully through political opposition to any U.S. aid or friendship extended to Israel. For decades, Closet Nazis came from both sides of the political aisle. Soon, many conservatives came to embrace the cause of Israel, and leftists began to dominate the netherworld of the Closet Nazi, as they grew closer to the anti-Americanism of the Islamothugs. As America and Israel's friendship grew, the Closet Nazi population began to multiply around the world, steadfast in the belief that Zionists were closing in on their ultimate plan of world domination.

BEHAVIOR

Closet Nazis are most nervous when attending a protest. There are always the questions, "Did my sign step over the line? How obvious is my Jew hatred? Will people really think I oppose U.S. relations with Israel strictly on foreign policy grounds?" These questions whirl in the Closet Nazis' heads. So they prefer to keep quiet as they strut around the protest march with sign in hand. Closet Nazis in general are noticeably shy at a protest unless there's an opportunity to be photographed. Simply point a camera in their direction and they'll snap out of their daze just long enough to pose for you with their sign (some specimens have been observed smiling during a photo, but this behavior is extremely rare).

USS *Liberty*

Every once in a while a Closet Nazi will engage in nonstop conversation at a protest when one of their favorite subjects comes up—the USS *Liberty*. On June 8, 1967, on day four of the Six-Day War between Israel and the Arab states of Egypt, Jordan, Iraq, and Syria, the Israeli high command received a report that its ground troops on the shores of El-Arish were being attacked from the sea. It was assumed that the attacking vessel was Egyptian, and was the same one that had shelled the troops the previous day. The United States had reported to Israel that there were no U.S. naval forces within one hundred miles of the battle zone. The American intelligence ship USS *Liberty*, after a series of U.S. communications failures, wandered into the battle zone and was mistaken by Israel for the Egyptian ship. Israel attacked the ship with warplanes and torpedoes, killing 34 of *Liberty*'s crew and wounding 171. Realizing its mistake, Israel immediately notified the U.S. embassy in Tel Aviv, apologized for the grave mistake, and paid reparations to the families of those killed. Closet Nazis around the world immediately made this fiasco their rallying cry, claiming that Israel maliciously and deliberately attacked the American ship. They are not deterred by the ten official U.S. investigations and three Israeli inquiries that have all concluded that the attack was a tragic mistake, exonerating Israel. Nor are they deterred by the fact that Israel would derive absolutely zero benefit from attacking a U.S. vessel (the United States was an important, powerful ally even back then). Nor do they give much thought to the fact that accidents caused by "friendly fire" are quite common during wartime, especially in chaotic wars where one nation is pitted against four surrounding, larger neighboring countries. Instead, they maintain that Israel used the attack as cover for its upcoming surprise attack on Syria or that Israel was trying to prevent the United States from discovering Egyptian mass graves or that Israeli commanders were ordered to attack by Plutonian mind controllers using an intergalactic space ship shaped like the Star of David. No anti-Semitic theory is too far-fetched for the Closet Nazi, as long as it fits the diabolical nature of the *Protocols* paradigm.

HABITAT

When not at protests, Closet Nazis spend almost all of their time on the Internet. This provides for an ideal habitat, as they are free to revel in their unalloyed perversity, and to do so anonymously. Other activities include endless debating over the Byzantine network of convoluted conspiracy theories about Jewish worldwide domination and the imminent extinction of the white race. A popular online destination for Closet Nazis worldwide is www.stormfront.org, a forum whose catchphrase "White Pride World Wide" attracts human scum from all walks of life. In fact, engaging a Closet Nazi on such online forums can be a great way to observe and interact with these specimens in the wild.

CAUTION

Any interaction with this species can have a diminishing effect on your faith in humanity.

CALLS OR SLOGANS

Zionism = Biggest threat to the world
Remember the *Liberty*!
Tel Aviv out of Washington!
The Jews already have their own country—it's called America!

BEST OF THE BREED: HENRY FORD, SR.

Aside from introducing the world to modern automobile manufacturing, Henry Ford, Sr., authored a book titled *The International Jew* (1922). This book has often been cited by Nazi war criminals as their original inspiration for entering the world of anti-Semitism. Adolf Hitler himself claimed he was profoundly influenced by Ford's writings. In fact, Ford impressed the Nazis so much that Hitler hung a portrait of him in his military headquarters. He was even awarded the most prestigious medal a non-German could receive from Nazi Germany.

Inspired by *The Protocols of the Elders of Zion*, Ford attempts to convince the reader that Jews are coordinating, with the ultimate objective of controlling the world:

"It would be impossible for any Gentile coalition under similar circumstances to attain the control which the Jews have won, for the reason that there is lacking in the Gentile a certain quality of working-togetherness, a certain conspiracy of objective, and the adhesiveness of intense raciality, which characterizes the Jew."

"The Jews are propagandists. This was originally their mission. But they were to propagate the central tenet of their religion. This they failed to do. But the mission idea is still with them in a degenerate form; it represents the grossest materialism of the day; it has become a means of character in whatever business they achieve a majority."

"As soon as the Jew gained control of American liquor, we had a liquor problem with drastic consequences. As soon as the Jew gained control of the 'movies' we had a movie problem, the consequences of which are visible. It is the peculiar genius of that race to create problems of a moral character in whatever business they achieve a majority."

"The fact of Jewish control of the theater is not itself a ground for complaint . . . however, there is the ethical test of how the control was gained and how it is used. Society is usually willing to receive the fact of control with equanimity, providing the control is not used for anti-social purposes."

The Nazis were so impressed with Ford's writings, their propaganda machine created the film version, titled *The Eternal Jew*, whose narration included: "Jewry is most dangerous when it is allowed to meddle in the most sacred things of a people—in its culture, religion and art."

Ford didn't seem to mind so much when the murderous fascist Nazi regime gained complete control over Germany's culture, religion, and art, and this control certainly was used for "antisocial purposes."

From the automobile assembly lines of Detroit to the slaughterhouse assembly lines of Auschwitz, Henry Ford has certainly made his mark on the world.

THE PARTY LINE

Our current foreign policy toward Israel is unwise, given the animosity toward the United States that it generates from the Muslim world. The Muslim nations have been provoked into war by Israel's aggression, and therefore have had legitimate grievances that they ought to address without our interference.

BETWEEN THE LINES

Jews are the scourge of the earth, and their nation must be stopped at all costs, even if this means that we support the Jews' sworn Muslim enemies. We must help wherever we can in their efforts to eradicate Israel before the diabolical Zionist plot to enslave the globe is complete.

HANDLING TIPS

- *Level One (couch commando)*—At a protest, show a Closet Nazi a fabricated "Elders of Zion" membership card. He'll immediately run home and log in to his stormfront.org account to announce his discovery. He will then be immediately reprimanded by the stormfront community for believing that the Jews would ever be so open about their diabolical plot.
- *Level Two (fairly concerned citizen)*—Ask a Closet Nazi if he enjoyed last year's Passover. When incredulity appears on his face, remind him that Christ was a Jew and the Last Supper was a Passover Seder.
- *Level Three (ProtestWarrior)*—Wear the ProtestWarrior T-shirt to a protest and videotape the Closet Nazis nearby going into an apoplectic meltdown.

SECURITY GOONS

CHAPTER 17

SECURITY GOONS

Security Goon: A self-righteous protest volunteer who labors under the delusion that he is on the front line protecting peaceful protesters from the fascist police, while attempting to clear the area of all dissenting opinion.

PROTEST SECURITY PERSONNEL/COUNTER-PROTESTERS CLASH IN WASHINGTON

By John S. Pappa
Johnny P News
10/26/03

The [ProtestWarriors] stood quietly holding their signs aloft. The signs, attempts at humor, had slogans such as: "Communism has only killed 100-million people, let's give it another chance, " and "Screw the Kurds, No war in Iraq."

Within 10 minutes of their arrival, security members from International A.N.S.W.E.R., organizers of today's Anti-U.S. policy protest, appeared and began to cordon-off the area occupied by the counter-protesters using yellow tape.

Within moments, members of the International A.N.S.W.E.R. security team began grabbing and destroying the counter-protester's signs, and aggressively shoving counter-protesters. A Johnny P News reporter was assaulted while trying to capture the event on camera. The reporter was struck in the head and his camera knocked to the ground and then kicked by a man standing with the International A.N.S.W.E.R. security personnel. The assailant refused to give his name or answer any questions.

IDENTIFYING CHARACTERISTICS

The most obvious identifying feature of the Security Goon is his bright yellow vest, making him the second most easily identifiable species, next to the Hollywood Activist. With whistles, walkie-talkies, a coil of rope, and an imbecilic look on his face, the security goon looks more like a roadie for a rock band than security detail. Security goons have so little actual responsibility in their own lives, and so little going for them, that they tend to overcompensate when given the enormous job of making sure people walk down a street correctly. That's why you will find them periodically checking things off on a clipboard, or getting angry at police, medical personnel, and other security representatives who actually have training and real jobs. Security Goons are absolutely convinced that they're responsible for protecting the hordes of protesters from the encroaching police state, a responsibility they take very seriously. The Security Goon has many jobs—seeking out dissenters for removal, keeping protester infighting under control, and destroying signs not to their liking. Although they are not allowed to carry any signage, they will usually wear an anti-Bush T-shirt underneath their vest expressing their solidarity with protesters under their protection.

THE ORIGIN OF THE SPECIES

Security Goons have been around ever since protesters began flooding the streets en masse. As Protest Organizers (see "Related Species" on pages 210–11) came to realize that someone would need to clean up the mess made by hordes of leftists, they began making requests for volunteers to fill this new "security" position. Volunteers would eventually come to understand and embrace their janitorial function, convincing themselves that they are, in their own way, contributing to a historical movement. During the protests that erupted after Operation Iraqi Freedom, the Security Goon's role began to evolve. As more leftists took to the streets, there was now a need to make sure they were marching in the right direction. Another role Security Goons grew to relish was silencing the opinions of those they did not agree with.

BEHAVIOR

Many Security Goons spend their time walking back and forth, agitated, wondering if such a protest and dissent could even exist if they weren't around to make sure everything went so smoothly. They derive much of their confidence from the bright vests they wear, and will become immediately hostile at the slightest perceived challenge to their imagined authority. The outburst of physically obnoxious behavior is usually ushered in by some sort of scream: "Move!" "Stop!" "Get out!" Security goons are quick to display outright belligerence, especially when faced by the police or people who may have differing opinions. Security Goons often fight one another for authority over the powerless mass of liberal protesters. For instance, International ANSWER's Goons will often clash with United for Peace and Justice's Goons for control of the march, each wanting to take credit during the press coverage. But nothing gets them frothing at the mouth like seeing a ProtestWarrior sign in their midst, which will usually prompt them into a

Figure 17.1: Security Goon silencing dissent

clockwork routine: Upon spotting the dissenting signs, they will begin to indignantly scream and curse, almost uncontrollably, at the Protest-Warriors, demanding that the signs be taken down immediately. After the ProtestWarriors explain the free speech issue involved, the Security Goons will then radio for backup. The other Security Goons, bored out of their minds and eager for excitement, appear within minutes and attempt to push and shove the dissenters out of the area. This is the point when the Security Goons will whip out their coils of rope and create a barricade, which the ProtestWarriors simply walk around. As a last-ditch effort, they will attempt to enlist the help of the police, who reiterate that pesky free speech issue to the Security Goons.

HABITAT

During protest marches some Security Goons can be found lurking on the sides of streets, where they babble harmlessly into walkie-talkies. The more heavyset Security Goons like to hover over the area near the microphone where they reassure Intellectuals and other speaking dignitaries of their freedom to rant into the microphone. Yet others like to stay near the Protest Organizers and police officers as they try to make sure the leadership is well protected.

RELATED SPECIES: PROTEST ORGANIZERS

Less obvious are those ostensibly in charge of the Security Goons—the Protest Organizers. Though they are distinct as a species, they look a lot like Security Goons, just without the bright vests. There isn't much interspecies variation in appearance or attitude. Male Protest Organizers usually wear slacks (Dockers), button shirts (wrinkled), and leather shoes (Rockports). The women will usually wear a blouse with a skirt, as most female Protest Organizers are too large to fit into pants. They may be holding a clipboard or a pad of paper with a pen. The most obvious identifying characteristic to watch for is enormous self-importance. Some see themselves as revolutionary heroes in the mold of Che Guevara or Fidel Castro. Most just see themselves as brilliant political strategists, street-level Karl Roves without a paycheck or power. They are assertive and opinionated and can dash off their talking points at a moment's notice while avoiding eye contact. Protest Organizers are conspiracy theorists, convinced that they are the focus of investigations by the CIA, the FBI, Likud, and all the major intelligence-gathering agencies in the world.

Protest Organizers spend endless hours in workshops and at training sessions to hone their organizational skills. They attend weekly meetings to discuss "social justice" and praise Communist dictators for their bravery in opposing U.S. imperialism. When not attending workshops or protests, Protest Organizers can be found at their respective organizations' local offices. These are usually located in a New York City class D office space donated to a church group that donated it to some other group that donated it to the protest organization. While at the office, some of them spend their time trying to organize mass busing so that leftists from neighboring states can make it in, or on the phone giving interviews for a public access show. But most just kill time on IndyMedia.org or researching 9/11 conspiracy sites.

REQUIRED READING

War Resisters League Organizers Manual. One of the bibles for liberal protesters, chock full of tactics, dos and don'ts—ten dollars plus two dollars postage.

HANDLING TIPS

- *Level One (couch commando)*—When you see police officers in a protest-infested city, shake their hand and thank them for their extreme patience and boundless sense of humor in dealing with the unbearably overinflated egos of the Security Goons protecting the citizens from "police brutality."

- *Level Two (fairly concerned citizen)*—Take a pocket Constitution and a ProtestWarrior sign with you to the protest. When a Security Goon sees your sign and goes into his fit, read him the First Amendment: "Congress shall make no law respecting an establishment of religion, or prohibiting the free exercise thereof; or abridging the freedom of speech, or of the press; *or the right of the people peaceably to assemble,* and to petition the Government for a redress of grievances."

- *Level Three (ProtestWarrior)*—Picket Protest Organizers' headquarters and give them a taste of their own medicine.

EMPLOYED WHITE MALES

CHAPTER 18

||||||||||||||||||||||||||||||||||||||||||||||||||||||||||||||||||||||||||||||||

EMPLOYED WHITE MALES

Employed White Male: A Caucasian male passing through a protest on his way to perform productive work.

IDENTIFYING CHARACTERISTICS

This accidental species among protesters is extremely easy to recognize because they shine out like beacons of reason in the vast nonsense of the protest crowd. You won't find any piercings, facial hair, tattoos, bright-colored or shaved heads, antiwar T-shirts, ski masks, keffiyehs, or unbridled angst among this species. Not at all. Instead, the most out-standing characteristics of this species are neat dress, good grooming, and a healthy, positive attitude. The Employed White Male species is extremely rare at protests, because most of them have responsibilities—families, friends, and jobs that prevent them from being involved in the time-consuming nonsense of protests. Most of the Employed White Males who are spotted at liberal protests have a surprised, shocked, or even dismayed look on their faces. This is because most of them are there by accident while making their purposeful way somewhere. Being polite, they allow liberal protesters to pass and politely talk with the Communist, the Anarchist, the Blacktivist, or whatever other species of protester approaches them. After realizing that he is talking to people with whom he has little in common, the Employed White Male makes his way elsewhere as quickly as he can, often exhibiting a look of quiet bewilderment as he tries to make sense of the placards, chants, and banners engulfing his neighborhood and accusing his country of racism, terrorism, and fascism.

Another important feature of this species that separates them from the rest of the protest animal kingdom, as denoted by their name, is the fact that they have steady jobs. Some own businesses and some are doctors, lawyers, stockbrokers, accountants, engineers, or members of the U.S. military. Some even enjoy working for large corporations. When not working, Employed White Males focus their energies on raising their families, enjoying the fruits of their labor, and passing the values of hard work, integrity, and patriotism on to their children.

THE ORIGIN OF THE SPECIES

Employed White Males didn't always seem so out of place at protests. In fact, Employed White Males were the original American protesters, rabble-rousers, and revolutionaries, who understood the necessity of collective action to secure their freedoms. When the British began to levy arbitrarily higher taxes on their North American colonies, the progenitors of this species—whose professions ranged from lawyers and judges to businessmen, merchants, shippers, land and securities speculators, farmers, scientists, physicians, and ministers—organized together to form a nation based on the inalienable rights of man. In a letter to his wife, Abigail, John Adams spoke of his future Employed White Male descendants: "I must study politics and war that my sons may have liberty to study mathematics and philosophy." And his descendants proceeded to do just that, building the most industrious and wealthy nation on the planet, earning the envy and scorn of the rest of the world.

As the leftist philosophies of nihilism and relativism began to dominate the late twentieth century, the undeniable achievements of the Employed White Males enraged feminists, Communists, and Islamic fundamentalists everywhere. Bound by the myopic view of cultural egalitarianism, the left insisted that Employed White Males not only did not contribute anything special to civilization, but in fact have caused more damage to the world than all other groups combined. And thus the Employed White Male was blamed for racism, pollution, world poverty, oppression, and every other wrong in the world. Today, he quietly carries this burden, too innocent to fully understand or be bothered by the contempt for his achievements.

BEHAVIOR

Employed White Males are usually polite, in contrast to most members of the other liberal protester species. They are reserved in their behavior and generally like to think before they speak. This may be why they have such a hard time communicating with the other species of liberal protesters, for whom there is no delay between mouth and brain. Employed White Males do not carry banners or literature. They tend to have a natural aversion to politics, committees, and bureaucracy for the simple reason that they prefer to get things done. They are not enraptured by the sound of their own voices, spewing venom at people who actually raise children, pay mortgages, and hold down jobs. Employed White Males are the happiest of all the protester species and don't have to suffer the embarrassment of continually being on the wrong side of history. Employed White Males can take guiltless pleasure in enjoying the fruits of capitalism and take pride in the accomplishments of their friends and family. This classic white male behavior, born of hard work and responsibility, annoys liberal protesters to no end.

HABITAT

At a liberal protest, Employed White Males can most often be found at the fringes of the crowd, staring in perturbed amazement at the procession or trying to talk sense with a liberal protester. Look for Employed White Males moving against the grain of the protest, trying to cut across the protest mobs to get to their offices, their homes, or their lunch meetings with business prospects. Some of the older, more seasoned Employed White Males don't try to make their way through the protests, but wait in doorways for the protest mob to pass by, just as they'd wait for a thunderstorm or a large cloud of noxious gas. When away from protests, Employed White Males can be found in offices, on construction sites, in auto shops, or anywhere else work is being done. They can also be found in homes, apartments, and condos, but usually after working hours. Sporting events are a good place to spot Employed White Males, as are the sidelines of kids' sporting events. The observer will find a lack of other liberal protest species in the normal habitat of the Employed White Male—that is, unless they are looking for donations or protesting against some corporate injustice outside the building.

SYMBOL OR SLOGAN

The American flag.

IN THEIR OWN WORDS

Employed White Males don't say much. They don't have to. They talk with their votes, and they support America with their dollars. Probably the most asked question on the minds of all Employed White Males is "Why have my taxes been raised again?"

REQUIRED READING

The Constitution.

HANDLING TIPS

Don't give the Employed White Male a hug. Don't buy him a ribbon. Don't spend any government money for a memorial. Don't offer to pay for his medical needs or promise him a job and a house. Just let him be to take care of himself and his family.

ACKNOWLEDGMENTS

The authors would like to thank the heretofore thankless efforts of those who had to endure the rabble-rousing (but necessary) shenanigans used to gather the raw material for this book. A special thanks goes out to our girlfriends, who had to put up with the ever-present pile of Protest-Warrior signs and camera equipment littering the apartment. To Brian Sussman, Melanie Morgan, and Officer Vic and the rest of the 560 KSFO Morning Show staff for helping us grow our two-man caper into a bona fide faction. To our agent John Talbot for helping us come up with the idea for this project and scoring us a sweet book deal and bragging rights at social gatherings. To Bernadette Malone, whose wonderful guidance and professionalism made our first experience with an editor much more enjoyable than one would ever expect. To the fine people at PersonalMaestro.com, for doing some of the tedious research work we were too busy to do ourselves. To Kfir's brother Golan who gave Kfir enough time off (unpaid) from his day job to meet the book's looming deadline. To Rob Haynes, for keeping the ProtestWarrior server safe from annoying intruders and helping us put the unsavory lads who head up the now defunct Internet Liberation Front behind bars. To Bill Crawford, for his tremendous contribution and creativity. To Philip Awuy, who drew some of the illustrations in this book while serving time in socialist Holland for protecting his daughter from local Islamothugs. To our friends Amil and Ensar Kabil for taking the plunge with us on our first protest crashing, swelling our numbers from two to four. To our parents, for not stifling our creativity as children by making us tidy our rooms. And to Jenny, for hanging in there even after seeing Kfir's salary plummet from high-paid Silicon Valley engineer to insolvent filmmaker.

ProtestWarrior
SIGN ARSENAL

EXCEPT FOR ENDING
SLAVERY, FASCISM, NAZISM
AND COMMUNISM,

WAR HAS
NEVER
SOLVED
ANYTHING

Communism has only killed 100 million people.

let's give it another chance!

★ WORLD WORKERS PARTY

...THE LAST THING WE ACTUALLY DO IS WORK

END RACISM & SEXISM NOW!

Kill All White Males

WHITE RACISTS FOR THE LEFT

1. High taxes and regulations keep minority upstarts down, protect good-old-boy network

2. Government monopoly on education keeps blacks in urban ghetto schools, prevents them from infiltrating our schools

3. Left properly recognizes blacks as inferior and in need of special help and quotas

4. Proud tradition of segregationists – only 62% of Democrats supported Civil Rights Act vs. 80% of Republicans

5. 50 years of liberal policies have destroyed the black family – Yes!!!

SUPPORT THE WHITE POWER STRUCTURE!
VOTE DEMOCRAT!

Protect
Islamic
Property
Rights
Against
Western
Imperialism

SAY NO TO WAR!

www.protestwarrior.com

BUSH IS A DICTATOR!

HELP SUPPORT
LENIN,
STALIN,
MAO,
POL-POT,
AYATOLLAH,
JIANG ZEMIN,
KIM JONG-IL,
ARAFAT,
ASSAD,
SADDAM
AGAINST, UH, DICTATORSHIP . . .

Socialist Action Network

working to perfect the ultimate police state

www.protestwarrior.com

HOLLYWOOD

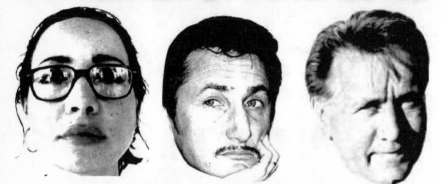

ACTIVISM

now *THAT'S*

Entertainment!

4 LEGS GOOD

2 LEGS BAD

A message brought to you by

Earth Liberation Front

Stop the Vicious Spread of Wealth Creation!

VOTE GREEN

and let's all be poor and miserable equally!

PALESTINIAN SUMMER CAMP!

LEARN TO ASSEMBLE ASSAULT WEAPONS!

WORKSHOPS ON LETHAL CHOKEHOLDS!

MARCHES AND HIKES!

TODDLERS WELCOME!

APPLY NOW!

(You don't want to be suspected of being a collaborator, so really, apply now!)

Scholarship grants from the European Union available, call for details.

INDEX